Inside the Principal's Office: A Leadership Guide to Inspire Reflection and Growth

Dr. Robert Thornell, Charles
Williams, and Michael McWilliams

DEDICATION – DR. ROBERT THORNELL

I would like to thank my wife, Sarah, for her love, care, and support during this process. She is the most passionate educator I know and as a former principal herself, she contributed many ideas, stories, and feedback to make this book as helpful as possible for campus leaders everywhere. I could not have done it without her encouragement! Thank you Love, we did it!

To all the principals I know and have worked with over the years, thank you for your help and for your commitment to making the world a better place. This book has ALL of you in it. An extra special thank you to the principals of my children's schools. You have a positive impact and are very much appreciated.

DEDICATION – CHARLES WILLIAMS

I would like to dedicate this book to my grandparents and my mother who were the consistent driving forces behind my unwavering pursuit of educational excellence. Their impeccable work ethic coupled with their passion for learning directly impacted the successes that I have experienced. I appreciate the numerous sacrifices that were made so that I could attain our dreams and goals. Thank you.

This book is also dedicated to my wife and children. Thank you for your ongoing support, patience, and understanding. I appreciate the many times you have allowed me to put in the long hours to support other families. I appreciate your continuous source of inspiration as amazing students and an outstanding teacher. You have consistently shown me what education can and should be. Thank you.

DEDICATION – MICHAEL MCWILLIAMS

I am thankful for my wife of 27 years, Shanda, and our two children Kenan and Kennedy. Thank you for your love and consistent support of me and my dreams. Excellence in all is our family motto and I hope and pray I have been an exemplar of that for each of you. This book is dedicated to you because you have seen me at my worst while believing the very best about my future. I value you, your support and love. It has made a huge difference.

This book is also dedicated to my "BIG BRUDDER," Greg, his wife Stacey, my nieces Kinsley and Kenna, my nephew Kyron, my god-daughter Ivy, and the many members of my village of support. You know who you are!

Finally, I dedicate this book to the memory of my mother, Carolyn Ann McWilliams and my father, Joe McWilliams who believed in me and taught me to believe in myself. I did not learn to read fluently until I was in second grade. They refused a special education referral and told me I could and would learn in spite of the challenges I faced. They showed me all kids can learn at high levels and I am forever grateful.

FORWARD
DR. EDWARD CHEVALLIER

The demands of the school principalship are immense. Principals are called upon to play a variety of roles for a variety of people — counselor, coach, advisor, disciplinarian, teacher — just to name a few. The list can be endless and often exhausting. And yet, numerous studies can be cited to remind us of the influence of the school principal on the success of students. Lest we need another reminder, a recent study from the Wallace Foundation (2021) included the following statement:

> *Across six rigorous studies estimating principals' effects using panel data, principal contributions to student achievement were nearly as large as the average effects of teachers identified in similar studies. Principals' effects, however, are larger in scope because they are averaged over all students in a school, rather than a classroom (p. xiv).*

In an earlier study, Louis, Leithwood, Wahlstrom, and Anderson (2010) investigated the links to improved student learning. In that report, they stated the following:

> *To date, we have not found a single case of a school improving its student achievement record in the absence of talented leadership (p. 9)*

A statement such as this reminds us of the incredible responsibility school leaders carry. While we always welcome the congratulations extended when our schools do well, we are also the first to be blamed when they don't. This 2010 study goes on to identify leadership practices that can be found in successful schools. The researchers state:

> *Teachers and principals agreed that the most instructionally helpful leadership practices were: Focusing the school on goals and expectations for student achievement; Keeping track of teachers' professional development needs; and Creating structures and opportunities for teachers to collaborate (p. 66).*

Practices such as these require planning, coordination – and equally important but often overlooked, reflection.

Yet, the principalship is lonely. As the authors of *Inside the Principal's Office* remind us, principals are on an island. After being asked to provide this foreword, I have spent a great deal of time reflecting on my own experience as a principal – and on my experience being named as a principal. The day after the meeting in which my appointment was approved, I eagerly showed up at my school in hopes of being oriented by the retiring principal I was replacing. As I was reminded (by him), I was not the successor he desired, so I was promptly escorted out the door and asked to not return until *after* his final day on duty. I'm sure any reader would agree that this constituted the antithesis of an orientation!

While this experience was a somewhat rude – or jolting – introduction to my new responsibilities, I have to wonder how many other principals begin their roles by being handed the keys with the assumption that they know what to do on day one and every day thereafter. The newness and immenseness of the job can easily be compared to stumbling through a dense forest looking for individual trees.

Inside the Principal's Office is a powerful title for what can be considered an incredible resource for any principal – new or experienced. The authors bring valuable experience to the task of helping principals organize and reflect on the responsibilities they face. As current or former principals, they know the challenges faced by principals today. It is difficult to adequately characterize this book. At times it reads like a handbook while at other times it reads like a challenge, an admonition, or even an encouragement. As I reflect on my own experience as a principal, I know it could have been helpful to me by helping me organize my reflection of a completed week and plan for the week to come. I especially appreciate the organization of each chapter with closing challenges related to instructional and servant leadership, learning, reflection, and celebration.

The planning, coordination, and reflection referenced previously require intentionality. The authors of this resource have provided a framework for accomplishing these practices *with intentionality*. I consider it a tremendous honor to have been asked to provide the thoughts in this foreword. I would be less than forthcoming if I didn't include my own reflection after reading the thoughts communicated by the authors. As a former school leader, and one who is currently working with experienced, new, and aspiring school leaders, I wish I had better practiced the art of reflection as it is outlined in *Inside the Principal's Office*. While our challenges are great, our opportunities are even greater. This book is a great resource for helping us realize those opportunities. I wish each of you continued success as you work through this book in search of becoming the best servant leader you can possibly be for your students and communities.

References

Grissom, Jason A., Anna J. Egalite, and Constance A. Lindsay. 2021. "How Principals Affect Students and Schools: A Systematic Synthesis of Two Decades of Research." New York: The Wallace Foundation. Available at http://www.wallacefoundation.org/principalsynthesis.

Wahlstrom, Kyla L., Karen Seashore Louis, Kenneth Leithwood, and Stephen E. Anderson. 2010. "Investigating the Links to Improved Student Learning." New York: The Wallace Foundation.

Available at
https://www.wallacefoundation.org/knowledge-
center/pages/investigating-the-links-to-improved-
student-learning.aspx

CONTENTS

ABOUT INSIDE THE PRINCIPAL'S OFFICE

School leadership can oftentimes be lonely and leave a leader questioning their judgement through challenging times. The live show, *Inside the Principal's Office*, was created by two career principals, Michael McWilliams and Charles Williams, to provide a safe space for current and aspiring school leaders to network, share, and discuss their successes and challenges in the field. Through their own reflective inquiry and efforts to grow and mature as leaders as well as a call to serve and give back to the educational community, the idea behind *Inside the Principal's Office* was born.

Inside the Principal's Office originally began as an online "show" where principals from around the world would interact with our two co-hosts, Michael and Charles, to discuss a variety of leadership topics. The show started in the midst of the pandemic, providing an important outlet and mechanism for many of us to connect during one of the most challenging periods educators have ever faced. The initiative has since expanded to include a robust Facebook group (bit.ly/InsidePrincipal), in-person meetup events, and now - this book, which is a collection of weekly reflections that we hope will be a useful toolkit for school leaders. We are honored by the diverse school leaders from around the world who have joined us in this journey of reflective leadership and continuous improvement.

Inside the Principal's Office is supported by SchoolRubric, a non-profit 501(c)(3) based in the United States with a global footprint that curates educational content such as articles, magazines, podcasts, webinars, books, and more in both English and Spanish. Its mission is to create an interconnected community of globally-minded educators in order to share best practices, stories, and trends in education. In addition to *Inside the Principal's Office*, several specific content pieces which exemplify its commitment to global education best practices include *InterACT Magazine*, *Global Education Insights*, and *Educators Without Borders*.

To learn more about SchoolRubric, become involved, or support its mission of connecting educators worldwide, please visit our website at SchoolRubric.com or follow us on Twitter, Facebook, Instagram, or LinkedIn @SchoolRubric.

ACKNOWLEDGMENTS

We would like to thank our colleagues and fellow educators Daisy King, Richard Siegel, and Adam Yhap for providing valuable feedback and support through the editorial process. Your roles and diverse experiences as educators across the globe in various roles have challenged and sharpened our thinking in the development of this book.

We would also like to extend a special "thank you" to the SchoolRubric and *Inside the Principal's Office* learning communities. The love for education truly transcends borders, and we have been inspired by so many people we have met along the journey who are doing amazing work with children. We have learned as much from your podcasts, articles, magazines, and other content as well as our interactions as we have given, and deeply appreciate the collegiality and commitment to continuous improvement as educators, organizations, professionals, and individuals.

INTRODUCTION: THE REFLECTIVE LEADER

Being a school principal may be the most challenging job you will experience. It also is potentially both the most rewarding and impactful position you will ever have! It can be an unbelievably stressful and sometimes thankless role; however, we believe you are up for it! We believe you can do it and we are here to help!

The premise for this book was birthed from the idea that we wanted to help principals be great. It can be a lonely job. Let's face it, just by the nature of the job **you** are the only one of **you** in the whole building. Depending on your community or district, there is a chance that you are the only one around for miles that knows what you are going through on a daily basis. If you are fortunate enough to have peers or a mentor you can talk to and depend upon, consider yourself lucky. The principalship is hard work and the need to stay motivated, encouraged, and inspired is what *Inside The Principal's Office* is all about. Following this guide will not guarantee you success, but we believe it will help you become more effective no matter if you are a first year principal or a seasoned veteran. We hope you will take this guide and change it, customize it, and make it your own. It comes from both our hearts and also our experiences of the principalship.

In his best selling book, *Good to Great*, author Jim Collins states, "We don't have great schools, principally because we have good schools...The vast majority of companies (schools) never become great, precisely because the vast majority become quite good - and that is their main problem." Our experience suggests that you will not find a great school without a great principal. Sure, there are many good schools and good principals all across the country, but for a school to truly reach its peak potential and become truly great for its students and its community, it takes an exceptional leader. That is why it is so important that you, as the principal, continue to strive to be the best you can be. It is your vision and commitment that will ensure the success of students and teachers.

So what is the recipe for greatness? The characteristics of so-called "great" or "effective" principals is well-documented, sometimes inspiring and other times quite boring. There are numerous studies and opinions of what it takes to be an effective campus administrator and while all of them add to the body of work to help school leaders, they also lead us to believe there is not a single right way to do things. Leadership styles and situations vary and our hope is that principals everywhere can stop trying to fit into a textbook definition of what a principal is supposed to be, but rather to gain confidence through small, personal challenges and self-reflection to gain insight on themselves and help those around them become better. The role of a principal is one of the most important and most difficult positions in all of education. It takes a wide array of skills and there is no recipe for guaranteed success, however there are some key actions that we believe will pave the way to helping any principal make a huge impact.

This book was created with you, the reflective practitioner and leader, in mind. Some who have read it think of it more as a devotional or a journal because it is not meant to be read straight through, but to read a little bit at a time, whereas others have found it useful to read through completely and use as a reference to consult with during the course of the school year. No matter what your preferred style, we hope that our collective ideas and thoughts challenge your thinking, affirms your actions, and inspires you to enhance the leader within you. It is different from other journals you may have owned, because it comes directly from *Inside the Principal's Office*. The question prompts and messages are written by principals, for principals. Every school year and campus is different, but they all have common needs and that is where we have placed our focus. As you read and reflect, it is our intent that you will gain purposeful insight about yourself and your actions and that we can help you be intentional about how you spend your time with some ideas that will improve you as a principal and in turn your campus as a whole.

In each chapter you will find:

- *A Message-* To share and collaborate with one another there is a simple message from a fellow principal or school leader with words of encouragement, inspiration, or challenge. Each message was selected to share a call to action.

- *Instructional Leadership-* A primary purpose of a school leader is influencing and guiding the instructional practices on a campus. This includes, but is not limited to, providing feedback, supporting teachers, designing and modeling expectations for lesson design, pedagogy, and accountability. In each chapter, you will find a different reflective question and/or activity for you to consider during the upcoming week. Some may be things you are already doing and others may be things you do not feel comfortable with, but in any case, they can serve as a reminder that can be adjusted to meet your needs. The important thing to remember is that you are responsible for the learning and teaching in your building. You may not be in front of students every day, but you are the "lead learner" in your building and it is important that you are actively involved every day.

- *Servant Leadership*- Now, more than ever, we believe it is essential for our campus administrators to lead with a servant's heart. Principals that are intentional about planning activities that can model servant leadership will gain trust and credibility from those they are trying to lead. Each week there will be ideas for activities that show a leader is trying to help and support. We hope you will use these activities as reminders and that some may become part of your daily routine.

- *What Am I Learning?*- A school leader needs to model life-long learning. Consider this section a personal accountability piece. This may be ongoing, such as a book study or action research project, but it also could be as simple as a quick tweet or blog post you came across that made you curious to learn more. In any case, the purpose is twofold:

  1. Be intentional about saving time for your own learning. You cannot be innovative or grow if you do not take some time each week to learn more about your craft. Be curious.
  2. Find ways to make sure your staff, and even your students and parents, know you are learning. Share with them. Ask them questions. Become a collaborative learner. Each week you will find ideas or examples of how to do this, but the important thing is to do it. It's not being selfish; it is growing yourself as a leader.

- *Tell Your Story*- How do you communicate with your school community? Newsletters, social media, stump speeches, etc. It is often an overlooked skill or task, but the principal is the face and the voice of the campus. Communication is key. Branding your campus is important. Too often, the great things happening at a school go unrecognized, but it doesn't have to. In this day and age of social media and the ease in which technology can be utilized, a principal should seek ways to effectively communicate both internally and externally with all stakeholders. Each week, there will be different thoughts and activities designed to shape the way you "tell your story" to others.

- *Celebrations/Reflections-* We encourage you to NOT be random with neither your celebrations nor reflections each week. These can be imperative to not only your mental state each week, but possibly those in your building. While celebrations and reflections are not the same, each week you will see an opportunity to do one or the other as a way to remember all the good things happening at your school, but also to deepening your learning through reflecting on the week and what went well and what you can improve upon.

We hope you will make your principalship journey personal. We urge you not to try and be something you are not, but instead use your unique set of skills and talents to continue to develop and grow. The questions, ideas, and activities we have shared are a compilation of years of experience, including failures, celebrations, and unquestioned learning experiences. Some of these are things we wish we had done better ourselves and others are the foundation of our success as campus leaders. They are shared with the hope of helping educational leaders collaborate and learn with each other.

WEEK 1: GREAT LEADERS LEARN

"Great leaders are great learners. They stay open to new information and the ideas of others and they are not afraid to experiment and make mistakes."
- Kouzes and Posner

Whether you are a first-year principal or a seasoned veteran, we hope that you start each day with the mindset of transforming yourself to be the best educational leader you can possibly be! Much like how an athlete or team begins a new season, each school year we begin with a clean slate as leaders. Your preparation is behind you and only your hard work, dreams, and aspirations lie in front of you.

No matter if this is your first year as a principal or you are a seasoned veteran, you are destined to make this school year the best one ever on your campus with your passion and your skills. As you read this book, look for ways to set a positive tone with your messaging to ALL stakeholders: teachers, students, parents, community members. It is time to be bold as a leader and let everyone around you know you are excited and ready to serve.

There is no "one way" to be a successful school leader, but there are certain character traits that tend to lead to high levels of success. As you move through each week's challenges, feel free to customize the questions to fit your style and your school's needs. However, there is a catch: successful leaders do not seek conflict, but they don't avoid it either. They follow their passions and their instincts, but they also know that to grow and learn, they must challenge themselves to go out of their comfort zone and they must be willing to let other people see them do so! Therefore, if you have to "pass" on one of the challenges, make a commitment to write down a note as to why you did not feel comfortable or did not accomplish it. Too busy? Not your style? This book is for you. Be honest with yourself and the learning and growth will come.

Instructional Leadership: Are you planning any new initiatives this school year? If so, how were they chosen? What does your staff need to make it successful?

Servant Leadership: What is something you can do this week to let your school community you are ready to serve?

What Am I Learning? What have you read or learned in the past week to prepare you for the best school year ever?

Tell Your Story: What is a piece of good news you shared about your school this week? How can you share it?

Reflections/Celebrations: What have you done this week in an outstanding manner that deserves recognition and/or celebration?

WEEK 2: ALL KIDS WILL LEARN

"Instead of giving reasons why I can't, I give myself reasons why I can."
- Anonymous

Who is responsible to make sure students on your campus are learning and growing as they should? As your school's lead learner, it is absolutely your responsibility to ensure all students are learning. However, it is also true that you are likely not in front of students teaching content lessons everyday which makes it both difficult and frustrating if you feel like you cannot directly impact students' learning. What you can do, however, is hire and train the best people available to put in front of your students. Hiring staff is probably the single most important activity that a school leader engages in, and it should never be underestimated or compromised.

The second most important thing a principal can do is lead a learning culture by setting high expectations for all staff and supporting them to meet those expectations. This includes not wavering when staff members cannot meet those standards. It is difficult to accept this responsibility, but it is necessary.

For years, schools all over have used the phrase "All Kids Can Learn" as a rallying cry to show that they are committed to helping all students. If you really dive into this statement, it potentially places the responsibility for progressing and learning on the child. Now, there is absolutely no problem with holding students accountable for learning and encouraging ownership, but what if just one word was changed in this popular phrase? What message would it send about the people you hire and the expectations you set if the phrase at your campus was, "All Kids WILL Learn!" By changing the verb of the sentence, you have shifted the responsibility to the adults in the building and you have also sent a message: "Can" means it is possible. "Will" is a commitment. A powerful, culture defining statement.

As you reflect on this commitment, consider your hiring practices. Are you looking for people that believe all students "can" learn or are you seeking teachers that believe all students "will" learn? One little word can make all the difference.

Instructional Leadership: What would your staff say you are looking for when you visit their classrooms? Why?

Servant Leadership: Can you name three teachers on your staff that naturally follow the "all students WILL learn" mantra? What can you do to show your appreciation to each of them?

What Am I Learning? Can you carve out one hour of uninterrupted time this week for your own learning or research? What topic(s) would you seek out? Why?

Tell Your Story: How do you share or highlight great teachers on your campus?

Reflections/Celebrations: Reflect on some of the best hires you have made. What characteristics did they have in common?

WEEK 3: SKUNK IN THE ROOM

*"A leader is best when people barely know he exists, when his work is
done, his aim fulfilled, they will all say: WE did it ourselves."*
- Lao Tzu

Over the last ten years, there has not been a more well-intended,
but poorly implemented educational practice than Professional
Learning Communities (PLCs). PLCs are wonderful and they
are not unique to education. Collaboration, team building,
debate, and discussion are all part of healthy parts of any
successful organization. PLCs provide a platform for innovation
and continuous improvement. Entire industries have been built
on the simple concept of putting a group of well-meaning adults
in a room and expecting them to somehow not only improve
their individual performances, but that of the entire group.

So, what is the problem? One of the biggest mistakes many
educators make is isolating themselves from people who
disagree with them. We often don't invite the "skunk" into the
room. Too many times, especially in education, we are overly
cordial. We view "debate and discussion" as an argument or
even worse, as personal disrespect. Without healthy debate,
however, your PLC will never be as effective as it could be.
When discussing ideas, innovation, or even student work, there

should be a "skunk" in the group that will be the voice of dissent or at the very least offer a different perspective or your PLC will never move past compliance level. There may be times that you yourself need to be the skunk asking the difficult questions.

The next time you are working with a team or group, look around and listen. Is there a person on the team willing to stick their neck out and challenge the status quo? Excitement and learning occur when we decide to create the future we need, not simply defend what we already have. Unless your team is willing to stay ahead of the curve, you will fall behind. We should allow the skunk to enter the room - our differences and the perspective of various members of the team are invaluable to the overall learning and success of the school.

Instructional Leadership: Consider the best PLCs you have on your campus. What do they do differently than the others and why do you consider them the best?

Servant Leadership: Sit in at least two PLCs this week. Can you identify the "skunk" in the room? If so, find a way to pat them on the back and acknowledge their contributions.

What Am I Learning? Find an article or resource discussing high-quality PLCs. What is your takeaway that you can implement or share with your staff?

Tell Your Story: Do your team leaders/department chairs know what you expect of them as PLC leads? What could you do to help them?

Reflections/Celebrations: Share something from one of your PLCs this week that makes you particularly proud.

WEEK 4: WHAT IS YOUR MISSION?

"Never doubt that a small group of thoughtful, committed citizens can change the world; indeed, it's the only thing that ever has."
- Margaret Mead

The most powerful thing you can do as a leader is provide the focus teachers, students and parents need to make the future better than anything experienced in their present. Our job as leaders is to provide an environment that is focused on what comes next. The daily distractions can make this challenging, but it is imperative that we manage the distractions and setbacks of our now and direct our learning communities to what comes next: the future. Each grade level is building a scholar who is prepared for the rigor of the next grade level. As an instructional leader, we are to empower and equip our teachers and staff members with the skills needed to meet the growing demands and expectations of the profession.

With all there is to do in a day, how do you cultivate a school culture that embraces continuous improvement? How do you motivate people to juggle daily tasks and commit to improving their practice to benefit the future? It is not always easy, but it can be done through a focus on your school mission. A school's mission answers the question "what does our school community stand for?" Our mission statements are carefully crafted and strategically placed on our walls and in our handbooks but do the adults and students in your building view their day-to-day work through the lens of your mission? Your mission is the reason why you come to work each day. It should drive every decision that is made. The fundamental purpose of our learning communities must come off the conference room walls and into our hearts and heads.

We all have mission statements, but on any given day can you walk the halls and ask a teacher, student or even a parent what your mission statement says? Could they recite it? Could they explain what it looks like in action?

Work to create a shared mission. Communicate your mission and purpose to teachers, students and parents every day. Use your school's mission to make decisions. Model what being mission-driven looks like and sounds like to your staff. When a mission becomes the focus in our schools, our priorities become more apparent and our focus becomes razor-sharp. Equipped with the knowledge of a shared mission, we can change the culture of our schools and school districts to increase student learning outcomes.

Instructional Leadership: Do students in your building know why they are asked to do the tasks they are asked to do daily? How are teachers connecting student learning to the real world, creating greater engagement and value? Visit at least two team planning meetings this week and probe the teachers. Challenge them to ensure students know what they are learning and why they are learning it.

Servant Leadership: Revisit the written mission statement of your school. Discuss it with staff members and get input and determine if it needs to be revised to better reflect the beliefs of the staff.

What Am I Learning? Spend an hour in one grade level. Visit each classroom and ask four students in each class the following questions:

- What are you learning today?
- Why is this important to learn?

Could they answer? Were they aware of the learning target? Collect data in the form of a grade level percentage and share this data with teachers. Celebrate success and identify what teacher behaviors are needed to increase student knowledge.

Tell Your Story: Your words matter. Commit to being mission-driven in your conversations this week. Let others know how important your collective "why" is by consistently speaking about it.

Reflections/Celebrations: Praise the actions of students and teachers that are aligned with your school mission. Each day, recognize a teacher and a student on the announcements or on social media. Others will begin to emulate what you praise!

WEEK 5: BAKING A CAKE

"Life is like a camera, just focus on what is important, capture the good times, develop the negatives, if things don't work out take another shot!"
- Ziad Abdelnour

Recently, we were chatting with someone considered a true expert in our field. We were talking about what seems to be missing in today's classrooms. It was **not** a critical conversation about today's classrooms. In fact, it was an acknowledgement that teaching today is harder than it has ever been. Students are more diverse, parents more difficult, both the content and the expectations have increased. Another variable that has greatly increased for teachers is the access and availability of resources. There are countless resources and ideas at educators' fingertips. A quick search of the internet or even the classroom bookshelf gives a teacher an abundance of great lesson ideas or quick fix strategies. Here is where our wise friend struck me with an interesting observation. She asked how many teachers know how to bake from scratch? And how many just make cakes from a box?

The premise was simple. We have all had some excellent cakes made from a box. You simply dump the contents in, add an egg or two, a little milk and PRESTO! You have a cake... actually,

18

you may have a pretty good cake. One that you would even serve guests and be proud of. The problem is, many of us have no idea how to bake nor the first thing about what goes into making a homemade cake. There is also no way we could teach someone else how to bake because we do not fully understand the process. We just follow the recipe. When an expert baker begins a cake, they know what ingredients to add, they put a little extra here and a little less there based on personal taste. Because of their experience and their knowledge, they know how to make the cake a little lighter or sweeter or whatever they want. They are designing it as they go and if you stopped them to ask, they could explain the reason behind each ingredient and the order in which they should be added. Sometimes an expert baker can take an existing recipe and make it better simply by adding a few pieces from their experience.

Teaching is no different. Just as bakers can design a perfect cake, so too can teachers design a perfect lesson. Teachers know the proper order to present information. They know when to add something extra and when to leave something out that is not needed. They know what is important.

Box cake lessons and resources are very necessary and can be very good. They help us be more efficient and feed our students. In a day and age when everyone is so busy, it is important to have tools that save us time and energy. However, it is equally important to have someone that knows the ingredients (the process) and can make adjustments as needed. Great principals search for and develop great teachers. They allow the autonomy and innovation needed to create a wonderful experience for students. They know we need teachers that are bakers!!!

Instructional Leadership: What are your expectations for lesson plans on your campus? Do they make a difference? How do you know?

Servant Leadership: Can you take a novice teacher into an "baker's" classroom this week just to observe a master at work?

What Am I Learning? Find a book (one you already own) and list two things you want to remember about it.

Tell Your Story: What might you tell parents about how your campus meets the needs of ALL learners?

Reflections/Celebrations: Discover a story of a teacher "creating a lesson from scratch" either for a class or an individual student and find a simple way to applaud their efforts.

WEEK 6: DON'T BE A CRAB

"Being positive won't guarantee you'll succeed. But being negative will guarantee you won't"
-Jon Gordon

Have you ever worked with people that go out of their way to make sure new things don't work? They don't want to put in the extra effort it might take to get ahead, either because they are afraid of failure or they are content to do things the way they have always been done.

Have you ever worked on campuses where teachers were actually ostracized for going "above and beyond"? Simple things like gaining praise for a great newsletter, an extra parent call, or even enthusiastically participating in professional development can sometimes make others jealous or even resentful. In some places, this is called the "Crab Mentality."

The crab mentality is a natural phenomenon that even scientists can't explain, but it almost never fails. If you have a bucket of crabs, they easily have the capability to climb out of the bucket and save themselves, especially if they work together. But they will not. Sometimes the crabs seem almost malicious. They climb over one another and even work to pull those that appear to be making progress towards success downward to the group. They are not interested in others' success.

We should all be on guard for the crab mentality. Even at schools with great cultures and climates, it can creep in and pull others down. If you look around your own campus and your peers, we are willing to bet that everyone there is working hard and trying their best. However, we also believe that there are a few that stand out. Maybe it's the way they teach a lesson with a smile, they make even lunch duty fun, or they have a way of getting along with that student/parent that no one else can seem to reach. The question is, what is keeping them from falling into the crab mentality? As a leader, the culture of the building is one of your largest responsibilities. Do the activities and tone you set create a positive and collaborative team atmosphere or is it a competitive environment that reduces the chances of sharing success?

The crab mentality is a reflection of the famous saying "we all like to see our friends get ahead, but not too far ahead." Learning to recognize the crab mentality in yourself and others is a very good idea, especially in schools. Our schools need teachers that "get out of the bucket" to seek adventure and try new things, not groups that are holding them back. Don't be a crab!

Instructional Leadership: Do you have a culture that holds "great" teachers back from doing even more for students?

Servant Leadership: Find a teacher that is frequently negative on your campus and volunteer to cover a duty for them this week. Don't say why - just say "you got them!"

What Am I Learning? Commit to subscribing to at least one educational blog/newsletter this week AND share it with your staff.

Tell Your Story: How do you share information with your staff? Consider a Friday "state of the school" each week.

Reflections/Celebrations: What is something or someone that has exceeded your expectations this week at your campus?

WEEK 7: WOW TO HOW

"Pleasing people is not the same as leading people."
- John Maxwell

WOW! Sometimes you can just tell certain things about a school. On some campuses, as soon as you walk in, you notice there has been this wonderful buzz of wow! It is the wow factor of ideas and possibilities that exist when we get excited. It motivates and inspires us to innovate and have the confidence to try something new. Maybe the wow comes from you, or maybe it comes from someone else, but every successful organization must have a certain amount of wow to be innovative and successful. Without the wow, we become complacent, content, and even bored. Celebrate the wow! Get excited about the new ideas and things you want to try this school year! Don't be shy! Be bold!

However...

After the wow begins to fade, every organization also must have a HOW? You don't have to figure out how to implement or solve the problem immediately, but there is someone on the team that ultimately asks how? For your campus to be successful in its endeavors, you need to take your ideas and make strategic plans on how you're going to implement them and determine their success. There are those among us that relish in the task of determining the how? These people are valuable and you should honor their contribution to the organization. At some point in the not-so-distant future, the wow is going to fade, especially if you don't have the how behind it.

It is how you attack your wow that makes all the difference!

Instructional Leadership: Does your campus have a wow factor it is trying to implement in classrooms this year? What is it? Do the teachers know how to do it or do they need more support?

Servant Leadership: Think of a time you rolled out a new initiative or idea to your staff with a wow factor. Did you intentionally include the how factor as well? Why or why not? Was it successful? What is the "how" your staff needs to make sure they accomplish the vision?

What Am I Learning? What is the last thing you read/learned that made you go "wow"? Have you shared the idea with anyone?

Tell Your Story: Consider your campus back to school professional learning. Is there something you could share with your staff that would help them reflect on what they learned with both the "wow" and the "how" in their roles this week?

Reflections/Celebrations: Think of a time you were very excited about a project or initiative that didn't go the way you envisioned? What happened? Did it have a "wow" without a "how"?

WEEK 8: CHECKBOOKS

"Look for something positive each day, even if some days you have to look a little harder."
- Unknown

As a principal, one of the largest responsibilities you have is the distribution of resources. Few things, if any, show your students, staff, and families where you place importance more than how you spend the campus funds. For some principals, it may be the latest and greatest technology gadget. For others, it might be extra books for students. Neither choice is fundamentally wrong; however, over time, your purchase approvals set a certain culture in your building. This is as good a week as any to make sure it's the culture you are intending. Some safeguards to help you are to ask yourself a few basic questions before you shop:

- Is this purchase designed to enhance learning and teaching or is it more of a climate/culture purchase? There is not a right or a wrong answer but aligning to campus goals/needs should be a major consideration.
- Is this a purchase in which input from others was solicited? Should it have been?

- Is this a purchase that benefits ALL kids or is it intended specifically for a special group?
- Are my purchases equitable among student groups? Grade levels? Departments? Or can I be perceived as favoring one group over another?
- Does my school budget mirror what I say is important on our campus?
- Am I prepared to follow up the purchase with additional support in implementation via time, professional learning, etc.?

Principals must be good stewards of their resources. These questions and others can help you self-reflect on your spending habits. As the old pastor proverb goes, "I can tell you what is important to you by looking at your checkbook." Make sure your books tell the story you want them to!

Instructional Leadership: What was/were the last instructional product(s) you purchased for your campus? Why? How will you know if you got your money's worth?

Servant Leadership: Can you find a way to spend funds that might show your staff you care about them? What might that look like?

What Am I Learning? Have you ever bought something for your campus and then realized it was not helping you meet your stated goals? How do you prevent that from happening again?

Tell Your Story: Do any of your stakeholders understand and/or participate in the budget building process? Who decides what is included and what is left out? Do your stakeholders know why?

Reflections/Celebrations: Remember and acknowledge "money well spent" on your campus. What was it and how do you know it was useful?

WEEK 9: H-DAY

"Never doubt that a small group of thoughtful, concerned citizens can change the world. Indeed it is the only thing that ever has."
-Margaret Mead

Have you ever heard of "H-Day"? Every year in September in Sweden they remember what they call "Hogertrafikomlaggningen" or "the right-hand traffic diversion." It happened in 1967. After several years of planning and discussion, the country decided it was time to switch to driving on the right side of the road (as we do in the United States) from the traditional left side of the road. The decision was made by the government in 1963 after years of debate and overwhelming opposition from the people of the country.

Why do it then? It was a change many opposed and it wasn't necessarily needed (although there were several safety issues) and it was going to be quite expensive. Despite the odds against them, the leaders pushed forward with the decision they were convinced was best for the country. In the end, they formulated a very calculated plan that included thousands of road signs, traffic lights, and road paint that all had to be changed on the one identified day. The entire country shut down on H-Day and all the work was completed. The chaos and accidents many predicted didn't happen. There were very few accidents and no head-on collisions! Drivers had been training for weeks and they were focused. The safety results dramatically improved, and Swedish consumers had access to more cars from around the world as well as alignment to the countries nearest its borders.

How does H-Day compare to school leadership? What outdated practices or sacred cows are we holding on to because it is too much work to push forward and make a bold change? What if Sweden had never had an H-Day? It wouldn't have been the end of the world. Sweden would have remained a great place to live and visit. However, maybe people are safer now, and maybe that alone was worth all the work. As an educational leader, you have the choice to play it safe. Safe can be good and makes people happy. But this story is not just about which side of the road you may drive on. No, it is about having the vision to make things better through planning, and the courage to do something different! This is a lesson to remember. When you believe in something and have the persistence to plan for it, there may still be detractors. But the change will be much likelier to meet your goals and not a head-on collision.

Instructional Leadership: Is there a big initiative or idea that has the potential to dramatically improve the learning in your school you believe will work, but it will challenge some staff beliefs? What are the pros/cons?

Servant Leadership: Could you identify one of the "sacred cows" on your campus and its biggest advocate? Have a conversation with that person and honor their back story. The investment in time may pay dividends down the road.

What Am I Learning? Reach out to a colleague or mentor and ask them about a change initiative they implemented and what they thought went well and what they might have changed.

Tell Your Story: At least two days this week, park in a different spot and walk in your building from a different entrance. What do the "other" doors tell someone about your school? What did you see and learn?

Reflections/Celebrations: Do you have a teacher on your campus that needs to be recognized or celebrated for trying something new?

WEEK 10: THE OPEN DOOR POLICY

"A genuine leader is not a searcher for consensus but a molder of consensus."
- Martin Luther King Jr.

How do you receive feedback about things on your campus? What is the pulse or the vibe on any given day or week? It seems as if most principals and leaders of any sort for that matter, endorse the "open door" policy, as they should. Often, they will brag about how they are great listeners because students, staff, and even parents feel comfortable stopping by just to chat about things informally.

There is no doubt that these sorts of interactions can be the sign of cultivating a culture of trust and comfort. Great ideas can be created and massive hazards can be avoided by simply listening to stakeholders and keeping your pulse on the climate and culture of the building.

However, a great leader must remember one very important rule: An open door policy is only as good as those actually using it. It is possible to fall into a simple trap of thinking "everybody" feels the same way as the one person barging in your office to complain about something or encouraging you to try something new. Don't fall for it. As leaders, it is essential that we intentionally and systematically seek out various perceptions and points of view in order to fully grasp the impact of certain decisions or initiatives.

What does that mean? It means your open door policy is only as good as the person(s) that walk through it! It also means that the door is two-way, and you are going to have to get out of your office and seek out those less willing to share their opinion. You have to train yourself to ask the question, "Who is everybody?" as a word of caution when those around you use it as a way of making their argument or plea somehow more validated. Rarely does "everybody" feel the same way about anything and a good leader knows this and works to determine the reality of the people he/she serves.

There are lots of conversations that can and should be had in the privacy of an office. However, never mistake an open door with the idea that you know what is going on if you don't have either equal representation coming through or if you make it a two-way door and go find out for yourself.

Instructional Leadership: Is there an initiative that a staff member may have complained to you about and even implied that others feel the same way? How did you respond?

Servant Leadership: What/who is the most underrepresented group at your campus? Who advocates for them? Do they have a seat at your table?

What Am I Learning? What is one thing you would like to know about your campus that you may not understand well? How would you go about learning more?

Tell Your Story: Think about three staff members that rarely, if ever, come to your office. Seek them out and ask them to share something positive about things happening on your campus.

Reflections/Celebrations: Have you ever been convinced to do something because you thought it would be a popular decision and then found out not everyone felt the same way? What was it and what would you do differently next ti

WEEK 11: WHAT DO GRADES TELL US?

"Learning is not attained by chance, it must be sought for with ardor and attended to with diligence."
- Abigail Adams

What do grades that your students receive on your campus mean? While you are probably not actively involved in grading assignments very often, you do play a critical role in the learning and teaching in your building. Here are a couple of worthwhile activities to lead your staff in when thinking about grades. First, ask your teachers or PLCs about the types of assignments they are putting in the grade book and possibly follow these questions:

- *Do the assignments that were put in the gradebook represent the level of learning tasks we aspire our students to experience?*

  Think of it like this, your teachers are communicating what they believe is important by what they choose to grade. We can argue all we want that it is the "learning that matters," but if we are using assignments and report cards as a means to allow parents to be partners in the learning, then the grades need to be a true representation of what the student has accomplished.

We should do our best to grade these types of assignments and disregard low level or compliance type grades. I am reminded by the old pastor's sermon... "You can tell what is important to someone by looking at their checkbook..." I would suggest the same could be said for your gradebooks.

- *Do the grades on daily assignments match up with results on district level assessments?*

  This is a key point. If every student in a teacher's class is receiving an A or B, but the student assessment scores are much lower, we must ask why. Is it a poorly written test? Were the students not prepared? A combination?

- *What is the demographic breakdown of our student grades?*

  Are the key student groups still the same ones struggling and what can we do to begin closing the gap?

Second, consider reminding your staff that parents and students should not be "surprised" by their report card. Yes, they may have access to grades electronically, but a phone call or email beforehand can be a wonderful way to reach out and offer support or even an action plan to our struggling students. Maybe just as important, you can also encourage your staff to pick a student or two that "overachieved" or worked especially hard and let their parents know how proud you are of their child. Little things like this can really be an investment in the relationship that you may need later in the year.

Grades and grading can be a difficult thing to do well. A principal that is aware of the practices of their staff and consistently offers feedback will undoubtedly help teachers and students learn and perform better.

Instructional Leadership: What type of student learning data means the most to you? Why? How do your actions show this to your staff? Students? Even parents?

Servant Leadership: What types of questions do you need to ask about the underserved populations on your campus? What do they need to help them compete with others?

What Am I Learning? What have you read in the past about grading practices? Does your campus's current culture align with your beliefs when it comes to student grades?

Tell Your Story: What story does your student learning data say about your building? How do you share your data with campus stakeholders?

Reflections/Celebrations: If you were to take a random look at the gradebooks of your teachers or the report cards of your students, what would you hope to learn about their progress?

WEEK 12: CREATE CHANGE

"Be the change you want to see in the word"
- Gandhi

You have the power to create change.

These are simple words that contain a powerful truth. So often we discuss how we cannot control what happens to us, but that we can control how we respond. But why should we become comfortable in being reactive? Why stop at positioning ourselves to be prepared for when situations happen? What if, instead, we channeled that energy into creating the change that we want to see?

While we believe that monumental shifts at the very foundations of our educational policies and procedures need to take place, we must also acknowledge that this is the same battle that has been fought for generations. A battle that has resulted in simultaneous progression and regression. To achieve meaningful and lasting change, we must not direct all of our efforts into addressing the system as a whole, but we must also begin making changes in the smaller arenas - our schools.

Therefore, consider the power that you have in your school. If you believe that our antiquated grading system reinforces an academic exchange system, one in which compliance and completion can be traded for high marks, how are you changing it? If you believe that the traditional canon of literature used in English Language Arts (ELA) classes does not reflect your students' identities, how are you changing it? If you believe that the achievement gap is actually a reflection of an opportunity gap, how are you changing it?

Yes, all of these changes need to happen on a much larger scale, but it does not mean that you cannot begin implementing these shifts in your own school. Why can't you begin focusing on mastery learning? Why can't you expose your students to cultural texts such as *Zora and Me* by T.R. Simon, *Esperanza Rising* by Pam Munoz Ryan, or even *Redwoods* by Jason Chin? Why can't you begin exposing your students to the world beyond their neighborhoods through virtual field trips and local or even regional competitions?

Realizing that you have this power can be both empowering and frightening. Knowing that you can, today, right now, begin laying the groundwork for significant changes in not just your students' lives but your own is exhilarating. Just beware the seeds of doubt - of not knowing where to begin, of not being experienced enough, of not having the resources - for they will grow quickly and tangle you up with their weeds.

Commit yourself to change, surround yourself with other change agents, and push back against those systems that, for so long, have dictated how you will operate.

Instructional Leadership: How are you ensuring equity of pedagogy and instructional resources in your classrooms? What can you look for and provide feedback on that moves your campus in that direction?

Servant Leadership: How do you cultivate a climate that allows for the power of change?

What Am I Learning? What have you read or learned recently that challenged your thinking?

Tell Your Story: Transparency is a sign of good leadership. Can you share with your stakeholders about a time you changed your thinking and why?

Reflections/Celebrations: If you could change one thing about your campus what would it be and why? What are you waiting for?

WEEK 13: DO YOUR BEST

"Doing your best is more important than being the best."
-Shannon Miller

At the onset of the pandemic, teachers were lauded for their relentless efforts to deliver high quality educational experiences despite consistently shifting mandates and guidelines. Eventually, those comments shifted from praise to condemnation labeling us as lazy and selfish as if working remotely was easier and thus preferable than being in our schools. Regardless of the criticism, we continued to be innovative and remained committed to our students.

Despite the facade of smiles and "I'm fine" responses, there existed a level of unprecedented despair, frustration, and helplessness. Maybe you feel this way. Maybe your teachers feel this way.

Nobody really knew how to navigate the crisis we were in. Yes, there were plenty of recommendations and suggestions for new best practices, but we were all learning along the way. There were no experts.

We do not expect perfection from our staff or from ourselves.

When we say that we anticipate hiccups and failures, we do. We have had our own as we have led through this pandemic and anticipate plenty more.

Consider the words of Jill Siler when she said, "big things happen when we take the next best step... over and over and over again."

Do the best that you can possibly do. Then do it again. Then do it again. If you do that, you will be okay. We would all love to be amazing. We would all love to reach tremendous levels of success. But we will also accept us being okay as we figure this out.

Coming back to Jill Siler, remember "that the feeling of being overwhelmed, and even inadequate, is part of the growing process and not a sign that you are not the person for the job."

You are where you are meant to be. Even if you are feeling lost on a journey for which you prepared for so long, you must continue to keep moving forward.

Instructional Leadership: What can you do to set the tone as a leader this week that despite the chaos around us so that we will LEARN and we will SUCCEED?

Servant Leadership: Can you do one thing this week that is unexpected for your staff? Something they will remember... it doesn't have to cost any money, but it should leave them with either reflective thoughts or wonderings.

What Am I Learning? In the busy world of day-to-day school life, it can be easy to forget your own learning. Pick out one topic this week that you want to know more about and spend one hour diving into all you can find about it.

Tell Your Story: Do the families in your school know what to do in case of an emergency? Are you sure? How do you know?

Reflections/Celebrations: Is there something that you are particularly proud of this week? If so, what is it and why? If not, what are you going to do about it next week?

WEEK 14: CONNECT WITH YOUR STAFF

"I've learned that people will forget what you said, people will forget what you did, but people will never forget how you made them feel."
- Maya Angelou

People do not quit their jobs, they quit their bosses. They make the choice to step away from a relationship that is dysfunctional and leaves them feeling drained at the end of the day. We spend a ton of time with the people we work with and as leaders it is important that we use our influence to create a culture of genuine compassion and connectivity.

It is not enough to ensure our staff is connected to a mission, vision and essential teaching behaviors. There must be connectivity between the adults inside your building beyond data protocols and duty schedules. The most engaging work environments are filled with people who have a level of connectivity that transcends "the work." In fact, the Gallup organization probes this level of connectivity on their Q12 Engagement Survey more than once. The Q12 is an instrument that consists of twelve workplace elements that offer proven connections to employee engagement and performance. The Gallup Q12 has been administered to more than 25 million employees in 195 countries, as well as in 70 different languages. Example questions include:

- Does your supervisor, or someone at work, seem to care about you as a person?
- Do you have a best friend at work?

Relationships are the currency used by every leader. Anything you accomplish as a leader will be done through the people you serve and support. Do not manage people. Refuse to be a boss. Be a true, authentic, transformational leader. Work to motivate and inspire others to see possibilities that may be hidden to them. True leaders create other leaders by connecting with them and building relationships.

Are you intentional with the way you connect with your staff or do you leave relationships to chance? Are you strategic in creating opportunities for your staff to get to know you and know each other? Relationships matter and Maya Angelou got it right. People will never forget how you made them feel. This is a very important task of leadership. Just as teachers are asked to create community within their classroom, community must be created campus-wide by school leaders. Small gestures like initiating conversations about things not related to work, giving handwritten notes and speaking to every staff member in the hallway by name go a long way towards building community. Take intentional steps to build deeper levels of trust and connectivity among staff members and watch student outcomes and productivity increase as well.

Instructional Leadership: What is preventing teachers from being at their best every day? Spend time this week probing your staff to identify their social and emotional needs.

Servant Leadership: What can you do to help your staff with non-school related tasks? Consider making a mobile car wash available to staff once a month. Work with a local dry cleaner to establish a pick-up and delivery service at the school. Provide a play space for the teachers' children after school. There are many things you can do to help teachers.

What Am I Learning? How well do you know each of your staff members? Spend this week having conversations with all new staff members that are non-school related. Get to know them beyond the scope of their job duties.

Tell Your Story: Share an interesting non-school related fact about yourself with three new staff members.

Reflections/Celebrations: Start your next staff meeting with a Good News Celebration. Ask staff members to share a personal or professional accomplishment from the week.

WEEK 15: HAM AND EGGS

"Leadership and Learning are indispensable to each other."
— John F. Kennedy

There is an old saying about a breakfast of ham and eggs that goes something like this: "When it comes to a breakfast of eggs and ham, the chicken is interested and the pig is committed." Roughly translated, the "ham" literally puts everything they have into it and the chicken is involved and shares some of the work by laying the eggs but also can go on to do other things themselves. It may be a stretch to compare or determine which one you are as a principal, but here is a little secret - you don't have to. Your students and staff already know your priorities and commitments by your actions.

As a principal, you have the ability to set the tone and culture for your entire building. You do this by the way you walk down the hallways and greet students, staff, and parents. People see it in the things you are enthusiastic about and the things that you celebrate. They also see it in the things you prioritize and the things you ignore. Even as a new principal, it doesn't take long for your staff to determine what is important in your eyes and most, if not all, want to make you happy!

Culture can be tricky, however, and it is something that even the most effective leaders work to cultivate and nurture every day. Being a principal is a 24/7 commitment and the stress of always having to be on your game can be hard and sometimes seem unfair, but it's part of the responsibility and something to consider when making decisions. As they say, it's part of the job.

As you think of the ham and eggs analogy, one place to consider your campus culture is when starting a campus initiative: are you 100% committed to the cause? Perhaps nothing is more polarizing on a campus than when a new idea is rolled out and teachers are asked to implement new things they question or are unsure about. When this happens (and it happens every year) perhaps you need to start with yourself and consider how the change is going to impact you and your staff. Your attitude and your actions will go a long way to establishing the impact on the campus. Remember, if it's important to you and your staff knows that, they are much more likely to believe and commit to making the project successful. All they need from you is a very clear and simply answer:

Are you involved or are you committed?

Instructional Leadership: What is something happening on your campus that you consider non-negotiable on your campus when it comes to instruction? Do you need to reinforce it in any way this week?

Servant Leadership: Is there an initiative or activity on your campus that you are not fully committed to, for whatever reason? How can you determine if you need to be more involved or committed to help others who do believe in it?

What Am I Learning? Challenge yourself to pick one thing that happens on your campus that you are not heavily involved in and learn more about it.

Tell Your Story: Pick three to five activities happening on your campus this week (in classrooms or co-curriculuar/extra-curricular events) and highlight them via social media. These types of things also share your "involved or committed" interests so make sure to balance them.

Reflections/Celebrations: Write down a list of "involved" items and "committed" items for yourself. What do you notice? Is there anything that needs more attention? Less attention? What would your staff say is important to you?

WEEK 16: LEAD WITH YOUR STRENGTHS

"Know Thyself"
— Socrates

The principalship can be a lonely job. Whether you are a first-year principal or a seasoned veteran, chances are there are times over the course of the school year that you may begin to doubt yourself and your abilities. Don't. It is not healthy or productive. Instead, we encourage you to remember why you wanted the job in the first place and to also remember the things that made you successful and allowed you to get the job. You are in this position for a reason, and it is always important that you remember that, even if it feels like others do not at times.

One of the characteristics many effective leaders have is the concept of "self-awareness." Self-awareness starts with being honest with yourself about your strengths and weaknesses. It is extremely important and it can greatly enhance your effectiveness. However, it comes with a catch. Self-awareness is only impactful if you are honest with yourself and not only your actions, but also your true beliefs. It can be easy to inflate your knowledge or skills, because after all, you are the lead learner in the building, but it can be dangerous to assume that you are great at everything. Likewise, a leader that is quick to shout, "All kids can learn!" but whose actions or comments do not reflect that belief soon loses credibility. You cannot hide who you really are from your staff for long.

To keep yourself in check there are a couple of habits you can develop to assist you in self-reflection. First, ask yourself what you are good at in your job. Maybe it is hiring, maybe it is data, maybe it is parent communication, or any other of the countless duties of a principal, but whatever you do really well, make sure you celebrate it. Most people thrive on things in which they find success. It fuels our souls. Knowing what you are good at helps you spend time on those things but also possibly helps you delegate tasks in which you feel less adequate to other people (perhaps you work with a team that balances these strengths?).

The next thing to ask yourself is what you are not very good at in your job. This amount of honest, self-awareness allows leaders to develop plans more intentionally for learning, delegate to those with strengths in that area, and also allows a certain amount of humility. These are key ingredients for successful leaders and leadership teams. By being honest with yourself about your strengths and weaknesses, it allows you to continue to develop, but also recognizes you cannot do everything by yourself. You do not have to be the expert on everything and the sooner you realize this truth, the more time can be spent on the things that made you effective in the first place.

Instructional Leadership: This week as you walk classrooms, focus on your strengths as an instructional leader and offer feedback, support, or help in those areas.

Servant Leadership: Have you considered teaching a lesson in a classroom for a new teacher so he/she may watch and learn from you?

What Am I Learning? Make a list of your strengths and weaknesses as a leader. If you are really bold, share it with someone you trust and ask for feedback.

Tell Your Story: Have lunch with a group of students this week and ask them to give you feedback on your job as a principal.

Reflections/Celebrations: Reflect on your calendar this week. What percentage of your time was spent on things you consider your strengths?

WEEK 17: FANS DON'T BOO NOBODIES

"No one can make you feel inferior without your consent."
— Eleanor Roosevelt

Hall of Fame baseball player Reggie Jackson was known for his big home runs and his big ego. He had tremendous success, but like the rest of us, he had bad days, too. As a leader, he had people that criticized the way he did things, but Jackson had a famous saying, "Fans don't boo nobodies!" He claimed he used that to remind himself that he was a great player and to block out the critics.

Now, we may not all have the same attitude as Reggie Jackson, but most leaders, principals included, did not achieve the level of success they have had without a certain amount of pride and belief in themselves. As a leader, your school community wants and needs you to exude a certain amount of confidence and determination about the decisions you make and the direction of the school. That does not mean they are going to always agree with every decision you make, but no one wants to follow a person that is indecisive or unsure of themselves.

Critics are everywhere. Staff, parents, district office, even students will all challenge you at times. Oftentimes they have the benefit of hindsight when something does not go well, and a scapegoat is needed. In times like these, you need to remember that "fans don't boo nobodies." When you accepted the role, it was not to win popularity contests, was it? Probably not. Instead of worrying about the critics or what others might say, you must always make decisions that are consistent with your values, do your best to rely on the information you have at the time, and at the end of the day, you need to be able to sleep at night knowing you did the very best you could have and let the rest of it take care of itself. Your number one job is to help students and teachers with their growth and development.

There will be tough days in this job. You will make mistakes. You will be criticized. Do not let those days define you. Stand up to the critics with self-assurance and confidently remind yourself that you are the best person for the job. If it helps, quietly whisper to yourself, "Fans don't boo nobodies!"

Instructional Leadership: Your goal this week should be to find at least five classrooms and rather than criticize anything that is going on, share a praise to the teacher regarding their instruction.

Servant Leadership: Consider hosting a roundtable of parents (make sure to invite a diverse group) and seek their feedback (even criticism) about things at the school. What would they change if they could?

What Am I Learning? Besides this one, what other readings are you currently involved with and why? Not what is on your desk or nightstand, but what are you actually reading?

Tell Your Story: Consider inviting a principal or educator from another school to walk your building with you and give you honest feedback about what they see. Don't be defensive by what they see or say. Listen to their thoughts and questions. Offer to do the same for them if they would like.

Reflections/Celebrations: Think of a time you received criticism you didn't agree with. What was it? Why did you disagree?

WEEK 18: IS YOUR SCHOOL BETTER BECAUSE OF YOU?

"That's your responsibility as a person, as a human being - to constantly be updating your positions on as many things as possible. And if you don't contradict yourself on a regular basis, then you are not thinking."
- Malcolm Gladwell

Is your school better because you are the principal? No offense, but the answer is not as simple as "yes" or "no." In a perfect world, EVERY school principal would automatically yell an emphatic YES!!! They would scream it from the mountain tops and their students, teachers, and parents would all chime in with a beautiful and deafening chorus of support. That would be a perfect world.

The role of a principal is one of the most difficult and important jobs in most school districts. This is not to take away from the work of teachers at all. To the students they serve and because of the work they do, they are irreplaceable. Teachers are saints. The principal, however, serves a role unlike any other. In addition to being the leader, at any given time he or she may also be a teacher, a counselor, a warden, a human resource officer, a social worker, a diplomat, a police officer, a cafeteria worker, an accountant, or any other roles as needed - and all of this may take place before noon! Here are two certainties:

1. **You will not find a truly great school that doesn't have a great principal.** It will not happen. Guaranteed. You may have great teachers without a great principal. You can even have great test scores without a great principal. But you will not have a consistently great school that works for ALL students without a great principal leading it.

2. **There is not an absolute predictor of who will and who will not be a successful principal.** Some people have the "it" factor and if we could bottle that and replicate it, we might just solve some of the biggest problems in education. However, there are a million different styles, circumstances, and variables that go into hiring, nurturing, and growing into a great principal that predicting success with 100% certainty is impossible.

So, if you believe, as we do, or you are at least open to the hypothesis of the two certainties above, then we must be forced to explore the question: **Is your school better because you are the principal?**

Instructional Leadership: Select the BEST teacher in your building. How does your feedback make them a better teacher?

Servant Leadership: This week, select five students and ask them to meet and share with them how proud you are to be their principal and why.

What Am I Learning? What did you do to intentionally make yourself a better principal this week?

Tell Your Story: What are ways that you share good news with your school with parents? Is it effective? How do you know?

Reflections/Celebrations: What impactful decisions or actions were taken at your school this week that you led or were directly involved in?

WEEK 19: WE CHOOSE TO GO TO THE MOON

"Some men see things as they are and ask, 'Why?' I dream things that never were and ask, 'Why not?'"
- Robert Kennedy

In September 1962 at Rice University, President John F. Kennedy gave perhaps one of his most famous speeches. It was there that he shared his vision to have a man walk on the moon by the end of the decade. It was a powerful moment. At the time, it was perceived the United States had fallen behind Russia in the "space race" and in one inspirational speech, Kennedy not only shared his vision, but he also gave the entire country a goal to rally behind. "We choose to go to the moon," he shared. "We choose to do these things not because they are easy, but because they are hard." What a tremendous statement! Obviously, history shows the United States moved forward and achieved the goal of walking on the moon in 1969, a feat that would not have been possible without the vision and the challenge to do the impossible set forth years earlier.

What is your moonshot vision for your school? If anything were possible, what would it be? Do you know? When things get busy, and they do, often the first things to get set aside are those lofty dreams that seem far away because they are not urgent and therefore can be dismissed as unnecessary. However, without big dreams, aspirations, and goals, what are you really aiming for as a leader of your campus? Try articulating it to yourself first. Maybe you can pretend to be writing a news article about your campus five years from now. What would it say? What would have been accomplished in those five years?

After you find your clear vision, it is time for the most difficult part: share it. Be bold and put the vision and the challenge out there for your stakeholders to hear and see. Your team might not see it clearly yet and they may think it is impossible but show them where you are going and why. Give them a purpose and they will follow you! The five years are going to pass whether you have a huge goal or not, so you might as well share it and spend your time working towards greatness! Indeed, work on going to the moon! We choose to go to the moon! Not because it is easy, but because it is hard!

Instructional Leadership: In the spirit of going to the moon, can you visit five math or science classrooms this week and provide feedback on their classroom instruction?

Servant Leadership: Spend some time reading to a class or two or go to a classroom and ask students what they want to do when they grow up.

What Am I Learning? What am I reading this week that will help me in the future?

Tell Your Story: What is your "choose to go to the moon" dream? Who will you share it with this week?

Reflections/Celebrations: Think of a time when you accomplished something very difficult or even something others didn't think was possible. How did you feel? What was your motivation?

WEEK 20: EATING IN THE HALLWAYS

"Children are great imitators so give them something great to imitate."
- Anonymous

On one particular busy day at work, a principal stopped into the cafeteria as he was making his rounds. The cafeteria staff always had coffee ready and something to eat.

As he left the cafeteria, rushing back to his office for a meeting, he started munching on a pastry. A passing student in the hallway jokingly called him out.

"Hey, are you eating in the hallway? You know the rules."

Before he could respond, a teacher, who also happened to be in the hallway, reprimanded the student for addressing his principal in a corrective manner. She felt that his behavior was disrespectful. After all, who was he, a student, to be speaking to his principal in such a manner?

The principal paused and thanked the student for the reminder - eliciting a surprise from both. He pointed out that educators, regardless of their titles or positions, should model the very behaviors that they expect from their students. As the leader of the building, he had the biggest responsibility for setting those expectations through his behaviors. If it was not acceptable for staff or students to eat in the hallways, then he shouldn't do it either.

We must remember that we, as educational leaders, are not above the rules, norms, and expectations that we have in our buildings. Instead, we must serve as the prime examples of those very characteristics otherwise we cannot hold others accountable when they are simply following our lead.

Instructional Leadership: What are you doing this week that will model the types of behaviors you hope to see in your classrooms for both your teachers and your students?

Servant Leadership: In your building, are there "unwritten" rules that some follow and others do not? Do you need to address this discrepancy?

What Am I Learning? Ask a few students this year about the "rules" of your school? Do they think they are fair and equitable? What about your teachers?

Tell Your Story: Do you have a story similar to the "hallway" encounter? How might you use the experience as a learning opportunity for your staff?

Reflections/Celebrations: Do you act above the rules you expect others to follow?

WEEK 21: ASPIRATION

"If your dreams don't scare you, they are too small"
- Richard Branson

Aspiration is essential because for so many of our students, their dreams are limited by their community. While they may have grandiose goals of prestigious careers when they are young, those dreams sometimes dwindle as the reality of their environments becomes more and more apparent. Ask any child what they want to be and you will undoubtedly hear the typical responses of doctors, or lawyers, or the like. However, it has been our experience that this same question often yields vastly different responses from older students. They, unlike their younger counterparts, have had their innocence stripped away and begin to look at the world with a much more "practical" view despite still being children.

This is not acceptable.

It is our job as educators to help our students aspire to reach their fullest potential in all areas. From academics to talents to skills, we need to encourage our students to raise the bar on their future possibilities regardless of their current situation.

How? We must first believe in our students so that they can believe in themselves.

Do you know your students' dreams and goals? Do you know what it is that they hope to achieve when they leave your school? When they become adults?

We encourage you to find ways to learn more about your students and then remain steadfast in your belief that they will ultimately reach their goals.

Instructional Leadership: What are your teachers doing this week to promote students' academic aspirations? What are you doing?

Servant Leadership: Is there a tangible way to share with your students the opportunities they dream of are possible? What can you do to cultivate this culture on your campus?

What Am I Learning? What data/information would you like to see that would allow you to gain insight on your students' aspirations?

Tell Your Story: How can you work to share the opportunities available for your students? Do your teachers, counselors, parents, and students all have a common knowledge of programs offered both at your campus and after students leave you?

Reflections/Celebrations: What programs do you have, or could you host, that recognize overachieving students in a manner that not only celebrates them, but also inspires others?

WEEK 22: ACCESS

"You never really understand a person until you consider things from his point of view, until you climb into his skin and walk around in it."
- Harper Lee

Aspiration cannot stand alone. How can we encourage students to dream big and then deny them the opportunities for those dreams to become reality?

Are you familiar with the phrase that talent is dispersed equally while opportunities are not? All of our students possess immense talents. The problem is that they are rarely afforded the chance to display them and thus they go unnoticed.

Consider a group of fifth-grade, African-American girls who were signed up for a rocket building competition hosted by Boeing. They loved science and talked about working for NASA. But they were terrified of competing against students from some of the most elite schools in their district. Nobody wants to be embarrassed. Nobody wants their dreams destroyed.

Imagine their pride and joy when they returned to school announcing that they had won first place. This would have never been possible unless someone provided them the opportunity to access spaces previously not available to them.

Consider the talents that your students possess and the opportunities that exist within your district, your state or even the nation. Are you ensuring that they have opportunities to shine? Are you providing them with the opportunity to reach their ultimate potential?

Instructional Leadership: How can you determine if the teachers are pushing students from all demographics to achieve at the highest levels? Are our expectations for student achievement high enough?

Servant Leadership: What support systems do you have in place to ensure students of all backgrounds have opportunities for extra/co-curricular activities, organizations, and clubs at your campus?

What Am I Learning? Seek out three to five students this week and "interview" them about both their aspirations and their support systems. What did you learn that can help enhance your processes for students?

Tell Your Story: Place yourself in the role of a new parent or student at your school. How would you learn about the opportunities and support systems in place?

Reflections/Celebrations: Can you seek out a piece of data from your campus that goes against the normal perceptions of students of color succeeding with support systems you have put in place? Celebrate it!

WEEK 23: ADVOCACY

"Average leaders raise the bar on themselves; good leaders raise the bar for others; great leaders inspire others to raise their own bar."
- Orrin Woodward

Aspiration and access are not possible without advocacy.

It should be apparent, now more than ever, that our students of color face challenges that some of their counterparts would never experience. It should be apparent that our students of color need to work so much harder than their counterparts to even be on the same playing field. Let us not shy away from this as educators, but rather, let us embrace the challenge.

There is a video that is being shared that serves as a visual reminder of how this looks. A young man shares that he is hosting a race and that the first one across will win a prize. The racers consist of both men and women of varying races. Before the race begins, however, he asks them to step forward if a phrase holds true. He then begins making statements about privilege. As you can imagine, many of the runners of color are left on the line while the others make tremendous gains though to no effort on their part. Consider this visual and ask yourself what questions you might ask that would create this same scenario at your campus.

There is an obvious disadvantage present and that is the case in our world. That is why we, as educators, need to be advocates for our students in every aspect imaginable. They need to have someone who is not only willing but is also capable of championing their future.

As the leader of the school, how are you supporting your students? How are you ensuring that their voices are heard and that their needs are being met?

Instructional Leadership: If every teacher on my campus were to become true champions for all kids, what would look and sound differently in our classrooms?

Servant Leadership: Many educators boast of support programs on their campus and community. Consider the difference between "offering" those programs and actively and persistently promoting and recruiting for such programs? If we believe they work, why aren't they full?

What Am I Learning? No matter what level you lead in K-12, spend time this week studying the demographics of your school and the results of each group. Go deeper than test scores and look at participation in such things as gifted/talented, honors courses, clubs, etc. Does the current reality match your own aspirations?

Tell Your Story: What role do you expect parents to play in advocacy for their students? How do you share this expectation with parents/caregivers on a regular and intentional basis?

Reflections/Celebrations: Think of two or three teachers who are great advocates for students. Take a few minutes and write them a thank you note for going the extra mile for students.

WEEK 24: YARDWORK

"The grass is greener where you water it."
- Neil Barringham

Yardwork can be a daunting task.

Depending on your own personal situation, coming into a school can prove to be a daunting task as well. If you have ever purchased a home, you were probably very excited. Depending on your price point or personal taste, many times the home will come neat and fresh - new carpet, new paint, even new appliances. And you hope it is perfect. It often seems that way. All except the yard.

Picture this: Before being renovated, a house had sat empty for a period of time and the lawn was not maintained. Needless to say, the lawn would be far from the pristine carpets that blanketed so many yards in the neighborhood. Instead, you find it has far more yellow (dandelions) than it has luscious green grass. The same thing can happen with an unattended school. Without proper attention, even the healthiest of schools can find itself in disarray. It may maintain many good qualities, but it will also have some irritating issues you will have to deal with. Let's call that yardwork.

Undaunted, many of you will launch into the process of domesticating your wild plot of land. You can cut grass, pull weeds, fertilize, and spray. Cleaning up a yard is not easy and takes time. It may take multiple summers as well as blood, sweat, and tears (literally), before you see noticeable change. The grass may be a little neater and there may be less yellow, but you may still feel inferior to our neighbors. School improvement is the same way. It is a process and takes time and persistence before meaningful change can take place and be sustained.

Here is a secret. We would love to tell you that continued hard work will help you discover the secret approach to maintaining those lush, picturesque yards; however, that would be a lie. Leading a school, while it definitely takes hard work, also needs more than just well-meaning and persistence. Instead, there are times when we must call in experts to help and they quickly are able to rescue both us and our lawn.

That may not be the ending you were prepared for. But there is still a valuable lesson to be learned:

It is okay to ask for help. Leadership is not easy.

It may be easy to notice the "spots in the yard" and make excuses as to why your students are failing to meet academic standards. It may be easy to justify why your school has a high rate of teacher turnover. It may be easy to criticize the lack of engagement and support you get from parents. It may be easy, but it won't result in change.

As a leader, remember that you cannot solve all the problems by yourself and sometimes you have to call in an expert to support you.

After all, the grass is always greener where you water it.

Instructional Leadership: Is there an area that needs your attention this week to improve student learning?

Servant Leadership: How do you model persistence for your staff and students?

What Am I Learning? Is there an area of challenge that you need to learn more about before acting? Where will you get that information?

Tell Your Story: How can you adapt your version of the lawn story to inspire your staff to remain steadfast to the challenges they face?

Reflections/Celebrations: Take time this week to celebrate publicly or privately a challenge you or your staff have faced and overcome.

WEEK 25: MODEL CONSISTENCY

"If you permit it, you promote it."
-Neil Barringham

When dealing with student misconduct, one of the phrases that many of us despise is, "well, when (insert name here) did it..." It is very tempting to, and we often do, respond with, "well if (insert name here) jumped off...," you know the rest.

In these situations, it is easy to hold the student accountable for their choices without considering the role of the school. Yes, the student made a decision to violate an agreed upon norm, but we must ask ourselves if those norms are being enforced consistently.

Are some students permitted to arrive late while others are scolded?

Are some students permitted to chew gum while others are reprimanded?

Are some students permitted to wear hoodies while others are chastised?

No wonder students often point the finger at other examples!

The same is also true for our staff.

As leaders, not only must we model what we expect, but we must strive to consistently hold others to the same standards.

Reflect on your current school practices and agreed upon norms for professionalism. Are all staff members following them? If not, are there certain behaviors that are more accepted than others? Are some staff permitted while others are not? Instead of modifying expectations to reflect behaviors, consider developing an objective system that can be used to monitor and address these inconsistencies.

Instructional Leadership: Do you have consistent expectations that are implemented when it comes to instructional expectations in the classroom? What are they and how do you know they are being implemented consistently?

Servant Leadership: Do all students and staff on your campus get treated fairly and consistently? How do you know?

What Am I Learning? If you were to ask three teachers and three students what the most important "rules" are on your campus, what would you learn from their responses?

Tell Your Story: What story does your discipline, attendance, and student learning data tell about equity and consistency on your campus? How might you share this?

Reflections/Celebrations: Is there a "norm" on your campus that is going particularly well and needs to be recognized and celebrated by all?

WEEK 26: PANCAKES

"You cannot be the same, think the same, and act the same if you hope to be successful in a world that does not remain the same."
- John Maxwell

Many families wake up every Saturday morning and make pancakes for their kids. Maybe they fry bacon (way more than needed) and get out a large bowl and prepare the pancake batter. Many parents have been doing this so long that they don't need a recipe; they just jump in and get to work.

Now, if you have ever made pancakes, you probably know that they do not always come out looking perfect like they do in pictures. Try as you might, to make them all perfectly round and golden brown, they still come in different shapes and sizes. Sometimes they are a little darker than others, or possibly a lump of batter that wasn't quite right. All of this from even the most experienced pancake maker!

There are several lessons to take from this weekly activity that are beneficial to carry with you into the work week. First, every batch is different, just like every child is different and every teacher is different. But different does not mean bad and rarely if ever, do you throw a pancake away. Instead, you have learned

INSIDE THE PRINCIPAL'S OFFICE

which kids like which kinds of pancakes. Some like them thin, some like them thick, some small, some large. Some even prefer weird shapes! Basically, you can find ways to appreciate the differences in pancakes and also find others who accept and expect irregularities.

Second, getting the heat just right is very important. Too cool and they won't cook right. Too hot and you will burn them. Sometimes it takes a few tries (You can call this formative assessment) to get them just right. It is the same with students and staff. Knowing the circumstance under which they best perform is important and if needed, you can make adjustments as necessary.

Finally, the other important thing to remember is just because you "know" how to do something and may have done so many times, this does not mean you will be perfect every time. Nor does it mean everyone will completely like your style. As the official "pancake maker" of the campus, it is your job to not get discouraged with irregular results, but to stay positive, learn from your attempts, be willing to make adjustments, and do your best to accommodate everyone's request. Ultimately, you have to ask yourself, "did everyone get fed?" If so, mission accomplished!

Campus leaders must always use activities and experiences as formative assessments and make adjustments depending on the needs of the school. It is not a weakness to adjust from time to time. It is, however, devastating to refuse to change because that is the way it has always been done. It does not work in leadership, and it does not work when searching for the perfect pancake.

Instructional Leadership: How do you react when a teacher tries a new strategy and it does not work the first time?

Servant Leadership: How do you work to accommodate the needs of various staff members? Is this a natural reaction for you or something you have to intentionally work on?

What Am I Learning? Have you recently discovered a new "recipe" or something you want to learn more about or try? What do you need to know to do it?

Tell Your Story: Do you ever tell on yourself with your staff when you make a mistake? Why or why not?

Reflections/Celebrations: Think of something that went well this week, especially if it was innovative or maybe an adjustment from the norm. How could this lead to an improved learning culture?

WEEK 27: DISNEY MAGIC

"First, think. Second, dream. Third, believe. And finally, dare."
- Walt Disney

Walt Disney and the corporation/kingdom he created have inspired millions over the years. Even if you have never been to one of the Disney parks, chances are very good you have seen one of its movies. Literally dozens of books have been written about the Disney corporation and how they create such magical experiences for their patrons.

Truthfully, the secrets to their success are not as much of a secret as one might guess. Much of it starts with a great culture and is followed up with hard work, implementation, and accountability. These things can get lost in all the creativity and magic that appears to the public, but at its core, Disney employees are focused on providing a unique and entertaining experience to its patrons and they challenge themselves every day to do just that.

At your own school, is everyone focused on creating that same sort of learning experience for your students? Walt Disney was often quoted as saying, "I don't want the public to see the world they live in while they're in Disneyland. I want them to feel they're in another world." What might that premise look and sound like at your school? Would it impact student engagement and learning?

As the leader in your building, you have a certain responsibility to allow, no - you have a responsibility to demand creativity and innovation in your teachers. Disney magic does not happen at the snap of a finger. It takes a tremendous amount of curiosity, trial and error, persistence, and collaboration to get it right. Professional Learning Communities (PLCs) should do the same thing for teachers as they design learning experiences for their students. The principal can model this in the way he/she designs professional learning for the adults in the building. They can recognize failures as learning experiences and they can celebrate attempts at creativity as they keep moving forward.

Too often, educators use the excuse of being "afraid" to try something new because it might not work or they might get in trouble. We preach that our students need to exhibit problem solving, creativity, and collaboration as necessary skills for the future, but we miss opportunities to stretch ourselves and our staff if we do not move outside our comfort zone or the limits that we think are possible.

When was the last time your students experienced a "Disney" moment? Maybe it is time to create one for them.

Instructional Leadership: Name the three most creative teachers in your building. How do they impact student learning?

Servant Leadership: Can you do something to create a plan that would make your next staff meeting magical?

What Am I Learning? Take one hour this week and learn about organizations outside of education that are considered innovative or creative places to work. Write down one or two things you would like to remember or try with your school.

Tell Your Story: Can you find five students and ask them about the most memorable lessons/activities they have experienced this year? What did they say? How will you use this information to inspire and encourage your staff?

Reflections/Celebrations: Write down the name of the best teacher you ever had. Why? What do you remember about him/her?

WEEK 28: NON-NEGOTIABLES

"People want to see other people who have 'non-negotiables,' things for which they're willing to say, 'This is it' we take our stand right here.' That's a leadership quality which people respect."
- John Ashcroft

As a new principal, one of the first lessons you realize (sometimes the hard way) is that you better know what you believe and why. Your beliefs and your opinion on everything matter to your staff. We have seen principals lose the confidence of the entire staff over things as simple as the teacher dress code!

Leaders must be adaptable and willing to shift their thinking when necessary. The school setting demands flexibility when dealing with "real" people and circumstances. However, truly great leaders also have foundational values and beliefs that will not waiver. These may develop over time and with experience, but no matter if you are a first-year administrator or a seasoned veteran, something will happen during the school year that goes against what you believe. It may seem like something small, or it may be a rather large and visible decision, but either way there are two things which you can be certain:

1. You will know it and have to make a personal decision to either step-in or not.

2. Your staff will also know it and they will be watching your reaction. It does not take long for your school to learn what you think is important and what you will let slide.

A regular test for every school administrator should be to ask yourself, "What are my non-negotiables?" What are the things that you are willing to take a strong stand on because you believe in their importance and impact on students? Some examples might include:

- What are your thoughts on student retention?
- How important are "jeans" days?
- Student conduct in the hallways or lunchroom?
- Small group instruction?
- Ability grouping?
- Student work displays?
- Teachers turning in lesson plans?
- Tardy passes?

The list can go on and on because of the thousands of variables in every school and that is the point. EVERYTHING cannot be important. The question becomes, then: what is important to you? Where do you spend your time and efforts? Your non-negotiables are the foundation for your leadership style. They are your personal beliefs about what you want your school to value and become. They may change over time, but do not be afraid to stand up for what you believe in. Be ready to share very simply that this is the way we do things here and this is why. People may not always agree with you, but they will almost always respect a person that stands up for what they believe.

Instructional Leadership: What is something your staff would say is very important for you to see when you enter their classrooms? Why?

Servant Leadership: How do your beliefs on staff expectations align with your actions?

What Am I Learning? Make a list of your personal non-negotiables regarding your school. Are there any you are willing to be flexible on or change?

Tell Your Story: In whatever format you use to communicate with staff or parents, is there a non-negotiable on your list that might need to be explained to increase buy-in or understanding?

Reflections/Celebrations: Consider a time you saw or heard something that happened at your school that you disagreed with. What, if anything, did you do about it?

WEEK 29: CLOSE THE LESSON

"The growth and development of people is the highest calling of leadership."
- Harvey Firestone

As a principal, it can be easy to assume that things are wonderful when you walk into a busy classroom with various groups collaborating on different goals. Collaboration has become a key goal in education as more and more teachers recognize the value of students working together to discuss and explore new learning.

One of the biggest illusions of learning can be a busy classroom. It takes an intentional focus by the teacher to ensure students are not only busy, but that they are all learning. The best principals encourage teachers to find ways to motivate and encourage students to be responsible for what they learn and how they articulate it.

Principals should expect teachers to insist students take responsibility and become engaged in a lesson. Once kids do this, they are much more likely to not only "go deeper" into the learning, but also retain the information. If they own it, they can share it! However, knowing the information is not enough.

Providing the extra opportunities for kids to share their learning with their peers is the final, essential piece of many lessons. Many of us call it "closing the lesson." As the principal of the school, are these the kind of classrooms you observe consistently? Are students truly engaged in their learning?

What many of us don't realize is that if we hurry through the end of the lesson or do not allow the students time to process for themselves, there is the potential to take away the student's ownership of the learning. Several warning signs:

- Does the individual student voice get lost in the group?
- Can a reluctant learner "hide" and let others do the work?
- Does each student feel responsible for the learning?
- Can one influential group member override the input of others?

It is paramount that principals remember to look for these indicators and provide feedback to the classroom teacher. An educational leader must be an extra set of eyes to help the students and the teacher be the best they can be.

Instructional Leadership: Visit at least three classrooms this week and ask yourself the four bulleted questions in the message. What did you notice about students being "busy" versus "learning?"

Servant Leadership: Can you cover a class this week or arrange for a teacher to observe another teacher?

What Am I Learning? What are your own views on collaborative learning?

Tell Your Story: How do new families get involved on your campus? Have you considered reaching out to them and getting some feedback?

Reflections/Celebrations: What was the best thing you saw in the classrooms you visited this week?

WEEK 30: LEADERSHIP EVERYDAY

"Everything rises and falls on leadership."
- John Maxwell

You are the leader at all times. People watch you when you are not aware of it. They make note of the things you say. Your every word is archived in their memory, and they watch to see if you will fulfill your commitments. Like it or not, you are the leader, and you are responsible for setting the weather in your building every single day.

It is the time of year when members of your staff may be exhausted, and it may be more challenging than ever to engage your students. As a leader you might even be overwhelmed, but that does not negate your responsibility to ensure learning for all students happens every day. To do that, you must be crystal clear about what is expected each school day. Have you identified the essential adult behaviors needed each and every day?

Create a culture of clarity in your building. One of the most powerful things you can do as a leader is to provide clarity for your followers. One way to do this is to identify your collective commitment together.

Collective commitments are the behaviors everyone agrees to demonstrate daily to ensure the vision of our school is achieved. The discussion and process of arriving at these common beliefs and a commitment to uphold them is powerful for any staff. By working through this together, your staff will gain further ownership in the process and the vision you are creating together.

In our profession there are so many things expected of teachers and students. The huge list of student standards and teacher tasks will overwhelm the best of us. Just as we work to identify essential learning standards for students, we must provide that same level of clarity for the adults doing the work.

Collective commitments bring clarity. Most teachers will give a huge sigh of relief if you collaboratively create a list of essential actions for their work. It does not mean all the other things do not get done, but it does let them know that the main focus of the school is the identified actions. They should be high-leverage and directly impact student outcomes. Give teachers grace and space for all other actions and tasks. Let them know you understand the huge demand on them and demonstrate your willingness to clear the path providing them the opportunity to focus on what matters most.

Instructional Leadership: Teachers know what kids are learning and why it is important, but do your parents know? How do you communicate current learning targets and grade level expectations to parents? If you do not have a system, create one collaboratively with your staff.

Servant Leadership: Ask teachers to monitor and document the amount of requests they receive from campus and district leaders and parents. Review the data and determine how much time teachers spend doing tasks that may not be closely aligned to your goals for student outcomes. Work with your staff to identify systems that can help meet the needs of others while protecting teachers' most precious resource: time.

What Am I Learning? There is knowledge within your district. Identify two colleagues and ask them how they help teachers prioritize the myriad expectations they face daily. Also, discuss how they prioritize their administrative duties.

Tell Your Story: What do people think you do all day? They won't know unless you tell them. Use your social media accounts and/or school and staff newsletter to share the things you do that impact student learning.

Reflections/Celebrations: What did you do well this week? How can you leverage this week's success to meet the challenges of next week?

WEEK 31: LEADING CHANGE

"Insanity is doing the same thing over and over again and expecting different results."
- Albert Einstein

One of the toughest challenges of our role in schools is the need to manage change. Educators experience constant change because best practice requires us to constantly engage in collective inquiry. To ensure all students learn at high levels we must be reflective practitioners. Reflection will always lead us to the identification of needed change, and it will uncover areas to improve. Honest reflection will shine a bright light on what is working that should be refined and practices should be disbanded. This reflection should allow us to strategically discontinue things that are not having the impact we would aspire them to have.

Identifying the need for change and actually leading a campus through the hard work of changing is not always the easiest thing to do but we must. There are times when reflection will cause you to question practices that are embedded in the culture of your school. Data tells us what to do and at times may require us to take bold actions to respond to immediate needs.

As you lead your staff through this process, remember to tell them change is not a negative reflection on the work they have done and their commitment to kids. If handled incorrectly, change can negatively impact morale. Do not be guilty of doing the right thing the wrong way. Be intentional and praise staff members for their service to students and families. Reassure them that change is about making steps to fulfill your shared vision. Increased student outcomes will always require us to change practices. A good leader will acknowledge how hard change can be and will celebrate the courage to think and act differently to meet the needs of students.

As you lead change in your building remember this: systemic change requires systems. A system is nothing more than documenting how we will do what we intend to do. Systems are to staff members as anchor charts are to our children. They provide support for teachers and guarantee equity across the campus.

Don't get stuck on the "what" needs to change. After you identify the area of change, work with your staff to create the systems of change. Make sure they are written and accessible for everyone. A written system will ensure equity. It guarantees all students receive the same things in the same manner. Don't forget to monitor and give feedback to teachers as they do this work. Support them in the same manner they support kids when trying something new.

Instructional Leadership: How do you ensure there is consistency across your campus? Do all teachers know and comply with campus expectations for literacy instruction? How about math instruction, handling discipline or meeting the SEL needs of students? How can you bring clarity to the things that are most important for all students to learn at high levels in your building?

Servant Leadership: Chunk the change process for teachers by providing benchmarks and look-fors. In fact, bring teachers along for the ride and allow them to identify these collaboratively. Together, paint a very vivid picture of where you are going and communicate often. Share where you are as a campus in relation to the big picture.

What Am I Learning? Consider creating a survey to gauge the needs of your teachers. Model for teachers and staff members how to use data to adjust practice. Use the data from the staff survey (formative assessment) to adjust one of your leadership practices.

Tell Your Story: Teachers want leaders who are authentic and communicate transparently. Share your journey adjusting to a change in the form of a newsletter article or blog entry. Let teachers know you are consistently making adjustments in your practice to benefit kids.

Reflections/Celebrations: Celebrate your staff by providing duty coverage to two to five teachers that are consistently engaged in your learning community.

WEEK 32: LEARNING AND DOING GAP

"I hear and I forget. I see and I remember. I do and I understand."
- Confucius

"Can you see my screen? Can you hear me?" These are questions that have become very familiar to all educators. The COVID-19 global pandemic threw us all into a virtual environment without adequate time to prepare, but teachers, students, administrators and parents did a tremendous job of learning new technologies.

How many PowerPoint presentations did you make during the pandemic? You probably lost count, but undoubtedly more than in a usual academic year. It became the go-to way of pushing information and "learning" out to our staff members. We were all inundated with information that was new learning and unfortunately in many schools, administrators did to teachers what we ask them to not do for students. We fed them large amounts of information without giving them the opportunity to practice, receive feedback or implement next steps.

There are two gaps that must be addressed in our schools. We all know about the student achievement gap, and we all have plans for improvement to address that gap. The second gap is not mentioned as often, nor is it addressed in the same intentional manner. It is the learning-doing gap present with the adult learners in our building. Our teachers are knowledgeable. We know a lot, but learning does not stop with the acquisition of knowledge. Our kids do not benefit from simple exposure to best practices. True learning occurs when we can consistently transfer our knowledge of what works best for kids into daily practice.

Everyone in our learning community should be learning. When orienting new staff members always let them know the importance of wearing two hats each day they enter the building. They are teachers/staff but they are also learners. For kids to learn more, the teachers that serve them must be constantly learning, acting, reflecting and refining. We are challenged to provide opportunities for teachers to become the benefactors of the strategies we use with students. In fact, teachers may implement strategies with fidelity as a result of experiencing the power of an activity as an adult learner.

Instructional Leadership: How are you supporting adult learning on your campus? Do you have a system that supports teachers as they try new strategies? What can you do to increase the level of support given to teachers? Identify the resources (campus and district) you can access to close the learning-doing gap on your campus.

Servant Leadership: Ask new teachers to identify when they will be teaching their best lesson. Outside of the official observation protocol for your district, go and observe them. Provide them with feedback that affirms them and that gives them next steps to improve.

What Am I Learning? You are a learner and learners are readers. Identify an area of leadership you want to grow, identify a book that addresses it and dig in! Consider reading the book with other members of the administrative and support team. Have weekly book chats during your lunch (when you get one) to discuss your learning and application.

Tell Your Story: Share your commitment to learning with your staff members. Consider creating a "currently reading" sign outside your door or in the signature of your email. People will be motivated when they see the collection of books and resources you added to your toolbox this year.

Reflections/Celebrations: Take time and write a note to all of the new teachers in your building with specific feedback about their contributions this school year.

WEEK 33: COLLABORATION IS KEY

"No man is an island."
- John Donne

When we started our careers twenty-five or so years ago, collaborating was not an expectation. There were few times we collaborated, planned instruction or looked at student data with other teachers. Oh, how we wish our older selves could talk to our younger selves! If we could, we would share the wisdom that time has taught us. Students learn more when teachers learn more. The collaboration process is an opportunity for teachers to learn from each other.

We believe collaboration time is where the magic happens in a school, and we have worked to make this a priority. Teachers are given time within their contract day to unpack standards, identify essential learning, write common formative assessments and review student data and artifacts of learning. Long gone are the days of teaching in isolation. We cannot allow teachers to close the door and exist in a vacuum. Make sure every teacher knows they are responsible for the learning of every single student in the building. Communicate this to teachers and students.

There is power in collaboration and as school leaders it is our job to make collaboration more than a suggestion. It must be an expectation. When teachers look at artifacts of student learning, they gain valuable insight on both student learning and teacher effectiveness. Collaboration time will uncover the skills kids need more time on, but it also identifies who taught what most effectively. When teachers gain this knowledge, they have the opportunity to be leaders. They cannot only reteach to the kids that did not get it, they also become peer coaches sharing the way they implemented the plans created by the team.

You may be thinking, "Wow, that won't work on my campus. Teachers take data so personally. There is no way we can collaborate at that level. We are not ready to share scores or kids." We have been at that point too, but remember this level of collective inquiry produces increased student achievement. It will be hard to initiate this level of collaboration, but difficult tasks usually produce the most rewarding results. Do not throw teachers in a room and tell them to collaborate. Guide them by creating protocols that help make the main thing the main thing. Make sure you are in the room when you begin a deeper level of collaboration and reassure them the process is about student learning and their learning as well.

Instructional Leadership: What do teachers focus on when they meet? If they are not talking about essential standards, what students are progressing and which students are not progressing, they are not maximizing their time together. Create stems, talking points, data protocols and/or an agenda for collaboration time. This is a great way to support teachers.

Servant Leadership: Show teachers you value collaboration time by showing up and engaging in the process. Ask questions and give suggestions.

What Am I Learning? Are you familiar with student outcomes in your building? Choose a grade level and review the latest assessment. Honor the work of your teachers by mentioning specific data trends you noticed when you see them in the workroom or halls. Take note of how their faces light up!

Tell Your Story: Share your commitment to learning with your staff members. Consider creating a "currently reading" sign outside your door or in the signature of your email. People will be motivated when they see the collection of books and resources you add to your toolbox this year.

Reflections/Celebrations: Identify two ways you can support a teacher who has students struggling to master a current essential standard.

WEEK 34: SOLUTIONITIS

"A genuine leader is not a searcher for consensus but a molder of consensus."
- Martin Luther King Jr.

As leaders, many times we become "fixers" of others' problems. We are often seen as the experts in the building or the decision-maker for difficult decisions, and therefore we are constantly asked for solutions. Many times, the answers are at our fingertips and easy to share. On those occasions, everyone is happy and for a brief moment you can walk around like a hero. Those moments, however, are usually very short-lived before the next problem enters the doorway and a new solution is needed.

While problem solving is part of the job and most of the decisions made are simply part of the day-to-day operations of a school leader, every now and then there are bigger problems or challenges facing a principal that require more careful consideration. It is these moments of truth that often make the difference between a good leader and a great one. The caution is to not fall into an easy trap called "solutionitis." Solutionitis is the idea or concept that problems can be over simplified or that a solution is given before fully understanding the issues in question. This is often done because of time constraints or possibly a need to feel like the expert in the room, but whatever the reason, the impact of a poor or quick decision can be substantial. Solutionitis has caused more than one well-meaning school administrator to make a situation worse rather than curing it.

Obviously, there are times of crisis or chaos when a leader must be bold and make a decisive choice without all the facts or the time to study the potential scenarios, but fortunately most of our decisions do not need an immediate response. The principal of a building has the ability to gather information from a variety of resources and be intentional about offering solutions to problems that may have lasting impact.

The next time you are feeling pressed to make a difficult decision, do not jump into a quick solution just so you may have a response. Instead, ask yourself a reflective question such as "Does this decision align with the values, mission, and aspirations of our school?" If the answer is unclear, determine what information you need to feel certain about the action needed. A principal cannot fear making tough decisions, but they must also become immune to solutionitis.

Instructional Leadership: Can you think of a time you made a quick decision about an instructional resource, practice or initiative and later wished you had taken more time to consider alternatives?

Servant Leadership: Is there a team of teachers on your campus that needs an appreciative "pat on the back" this week? What can you do to show your appreciation?

What Am I Learning? Is there an upcoming decision that requires you to do a little research or studying? What is it and what information do you need to make an informed decision?

Tell Your Story: Can you use your next staff or family communication to ask for some feedback or input about your school? How often do you seek input from others and how do you use feedback to make decisions?

Reflections/Celebrations: Have students from a few different classes to share with you what they like best about your school. Share their responses with your staff.

WEEK 35: 85/15/5

"Deciding what not to do is as important as deciding what to do."
— Jessica Jackley

You are the leader of your school; it is important that you discern what you bring to your learning environment. Confidence in knowing what you do best is crucial to your success. Years ago, when we became school leaders, we thought we had to do everything, make every decision and be everywhere at the same time. Years later, we now realize it is impossible to fulfill our responsibility of creating new leaders if we do not delegate and allow others to experience difficult decisions.

At times it is easy to believe tasks such as desegregating the data, writing plans, creating all the schedules and completing a myriad of other tasks is what you have to do to be a "good principal." You do not have to do it all. You may realize that doing everything robs the people from growing. It can also rob yourself of energy and create a pace you cannot maintain.

If you are at this point, we recommend the book *Leading on Empty* by Wayne Cordeiro. It can be life-changing if you are at the apex of burnout because it introduces the 85/15/5 concept. This concept helps share that 85 percent of the things we do as leaders anyone can do while 15 percent of the things that consume our time could be done by someone else if we took the time to train and mentor them. This leaves five percent and it is that five percent that is unique to our role as transformational leaders.

Work to spend the bulk of your time doing what matters most and is closely aligned to your personal mission. We have mission statements for our schools. We know why our schools exist. Have you done that work personally? It is important for you to be aware of why you exist and the specific contribution you exist to make in your building. How are you impacting student and adult learning? What impact should you be making within the community you serve? Identify your mission, your five percent and prioritize your time.

Letting go is difficult, but it is imperative. Take time to identify staff members who want to be leaders and invest time in them. Build their leadership capacity by giving them the opportunity to make decisions, create plans and lead. Train and mentor them and they will become an authentic voice that is needed in your building instead of a mere echo of you. You will create an atmosphere of synergy and produce higher levels of staff engagement and for yourself!

Instructional Leadership: Who are the potential leaders in your building? Identify them and share a recent article or resource that can help them grow their leadership. Remember to follow up with them and ask them their thoughts about their reading.

Servant Leadership: Are staff members aware of their individual strengths? Do they know what unique qualities they bring to their grade level team and the school community? Ask every staff member to create a list of what they believe are their top strengths.

What Am I Learning? Consider using a survey to collect the strengths of each staff member. Review it and use it to create teams, committees and other campus groups.

Tell Your Story: Share your personal mission statement with your staff in writing, through email or your newsletter. Let them know what tasks you prioritize as a result of your personal mission.

Reflections/Celebrations: Create a display (or delegate the task) that highlights and celebrates staff member strengths.

WEEK 36: AUTHENTIC PLCS

"The main thing is to keep the main thing the main thing."
- Stephen Covey

Every day of the school year, parents trust us with their children. When they send their most precious possession, their child, to us each day, they are communicating their trust in the adults in our buildings. We are the recipients of students and we are the recipients of the hopes, dreams and expectations of parents. They trust us to provide an environment that is safe and one that is conducive to learning.

There are now many educational options. Parents can choose to homeschool or enroll their children in virtual schools. Charter schools and co-ops are options in many areas as well. The parents we serve have made the decision that our school is the best option for their child to learn. Because of this, it is imperative that we keep the main thing the main thing: focused on student learning.

All students can learn at high levels. For this to be a reality in your building you must use your influence to cultivate an environment that is committed to doing whatever it takes to see all kids learn at high levels. The most powerful way to make sure

111

this happens is by becoming a Professional Learning Community (PLC).

Did you catch that? PLC is not something you do. PLC is what you become. In a true Professional Learning Community, learning is not an option for the teachers or the students they serve. Everyone is obligated to learn and improve because the adults in the building understand student learning is their primary responsibility. As a result, we cannot be satisfied with knowing we offered the opportunity for students to learn. Satisfaction should only come from knowing our energy went into ensuring all students can demonstrate mastery of the skills identified as essential for their grade level.

Do you have the structures in place to ensure students are taught and actually learn? As the leader of your learning community, it is your responsibility to keep the focus on student learning. Remember, the best way to ensure students are learning is to provide quality learning experiences for the adults that influence them. Both staff members (notice we did not say teachers) and parents should be learning. Students learn more when the adults learn more.

Remember, each day a student is in our building we should move them one day closer to the things they want to be when they grow up. Our schools should be confident kids are growing and when data suggest they are not there must be a systematic response.

Instructional Leadership: How does your campus respond when students are not learning? What research-based strategies are used to intervene?

Servant Leadership: Do staff members have job-embedded learning opportunities on your campus? Identify teachers who would benefit from a strong example and cover their class so they can observe in the classroom of another teacher.

What Am I Learning? Spend time in the classrooms of three of your strongest teachers. Identify first-hand what they do to get results. Share what you see with other teachers by highlighting them in your newsletter and conversations with others.

Tell Your Story: Are there teachers in need of support on your campus? Communicate your concerns to them and to your support staff. Make sure instructional coaches, specialists and other available staff members are aware. Rally every resource available to ensure these teachers do not fail. When teachers fail, students fail.

Reflections/Celebrations: Everyone can benefit from a mentor. Do you have one? Identify a leader that can help you grow. Follow them on Twitter, send them an email asking how they would approach a problem, ask them to review student data with you or identify another way to glean from their wisdom and experience.

WEEK 37: CO-PRINCIPALSHIP

"Become the kind of leader that people would follow voluntarily; even if you had no title or position."
- Brian Tracy

In education, we speak against labeling kids while being attached to the labels we put on ourselves. How many times have you heard, "I'm just a teacher?" or "I'm just the assistant principal (AP)?" Have you ever had someone enter the doors of the office and refuse to see anyone but the principal? What would happen if you worked to change the expectations of principals and assistant principals? How could you serve your campus better if you formed a partnership and established a "co-principal" relationship and team?

Our charge is to enter the building each day and ensure students have access to quality tier one instruction coupled with appropriate extensions and/or tier two interventions. The weight of that responsibility surpasses the limitation traditional titles place on the people under the roof of our schools. Our goal has been to erase the lines that separate principals and assistant principals. Everyone in our building is a leader and true leadership does not require a title, an office, a name plate or business card. What it does require is a deep conviction in mission and purpose. Mission-minded people do not care about the title, but they will always be found pursuing a purpose. They focus on every kid every day and they see each win as a win for the collaborative team. Mission-minded people seek to clarify what kids should be learning each and every day, create systems that help identify what learning has taken place and develop appropriate plans for kids who mastered essential skills and respond with urgency to those who did not. Mission is at the core of the co-principal model. All parties must be passionate about student learning and willing to invest time and effort in ensuring learning for all students. There is a clear difference in the salary for both of these roles, but mission-minded people will overcome this challenge by placing more value on the reward of increased student outcomes.

When done well, developing the "co-principalship" model will help you move toward your school's vision which should be centered around the learning of every student every day. A co-principal approach to leadership abandons the traditional responsibilities of each title and divides the work based on the strengths of each individual. While this term is not used in our daily conversations, it is the foundation of our administrative team and the way we approach our work each day.

Take a few moments and reflect on the impact of your current leadership team. Challenge yourself to reflect on the level of student learning in your building. Are you leveraging your strengths for students? Work to identify ways leadership can be more distributed, shared and collaborative.

Instructional Leadership: What is your strength? What are the strengths of your counterpart? How will these different strengths help kids learn at higher levels?

Servant Leadership: This week seek the assistance of another administrator on your campus who has a strength you do not. Ask them help give you feedback about a project you are working on.

What Am I Learning? Identify the strengths of each teacher on one of your teams. Lead a conversation with the team and learn how they feel they can use their strengths to help kids learn at higher levels.

Tell Your Story: Create a spreadsheet that communicates the roles and responsibilities of each member of the administrative team and support staff and discuss it with staff members. Teachers need to know who does what and where to get the help they need.

Reflections/Celebrations: Teachers do not always see themselves as leaders. What can you do to help them realize they are? Identify tasks and opportunities this week and let them lead.

WEEK 38: SHADOW A STUDENT

"In order to empathize with someone's experience you must be willing to believe them as they see it, and not how you imagine their experience to be."
- Brené Brown

How often do you reflect or consider your students' experience at your school? Often, we busy ourselves with making sure everyone is safe, happy, and learning, but are we able to truly visualize the school day from the eyes of one of your students? Some things you might consider:

- Is there anyone greeting them in the morning that knows their name?
- Do they feel welcome in the hallway as they enter the building?
- Do they speak to an adult in a meaningful way?

Once a student is safely inside your school and their learning day begins, what happens next? Are rituals and routines established that allow all students to know what is expected of them? Many schools establish things like morning meetings in classrooms or some sort of check-in time and these things are well intended, but what does it look like in the eyes of the students? Who participates? And more importantly, who doesn't? It takes a true expert teacher to touch base with every child, every day. It must be an intentional part of the daily routine.

Beyond greetings and morning meetings, what does the actual learning time look like for students on your campus? Are they engaged with the kind of content and pedagogy we imagine or are they bored? When you enter classrooms, are their kids collaborating with the teacher and each other while others sit silently?

One activity, no matter what grade levels are on your campus, you can do to learn a lot about your school through the eyes of a student is simple: shadow a student. Challenge yourself to spend a full day following one particular student throughout the day. Follow their schedule, eat lunch, go to recess, do the same assignments, interact with their friends. This might seem uncomfortable at first (for you, for them, and probably for their teachers) but we believe every principal should do this at least once a year. The time is well worth the investment and the learning could change your perspective. The worst thing that could happen is you spend a day with a student and what could possibly be wrong with that?

Instructional Leadership: If you were to shadow a student for a full day, can you determine what percentage of time was spent on authentic learning?

Servant Leadership: Is it possible for a student on your campus to go a full day without having a one-on-one interaction with an adult?

What Am I Learning? Ask at least five students this week to finish this sentence, "I wish my teacher knew..." It will be even more powerful if you have them write it out.

Tell Your Story: Commit to sharing about your day shadowing a student with your staff and any other possible stakeholders. Be transparent about your experience.

Reflections/Celebrations: No matter what you say when shadowing a student, write the teachers a thank you expressing your gratitude.

WEEK 39: WALKING AROUND

"An organization, no matter how well designed, is only as good as the
people who live and work in it."
- Dee Hock

We don't know much about cars. We can change a tire, plug a
flat, check the oil, but our skills typically don't go much further
than these basic feats. Despite these limitations, we know that
each component, regardless of its role, is critical to ensuring that
the entire car functions.

Schools are no different.

As leaders, we must recognize the various staff members in our
buildings and take the time to ensure that each is operating as
effectively and efficiently as possible. This cannot be done from
our offices. This cannot be done with an email or a memo.
Instead, we must make the time to personally invest in each
person within our organization.

Every morning, before students even arrive, we take a walk
through our schools. Not only does it give us an opportunity to
collect our thoughts and to check on the status of the building,
but it also gives us the chance to connect our staff. We will pop

into classrooms as teachers are setting up to chat or even help them organize their desks. We'll check on our building engineer to see how his family is doing (we have a lot of parallels!). We greet the cafeteria staff and commend them on the smells coming from the kitchen.

These brief, yet consistent, interactions allow us the opportunity to connect with our staff and to personally check-in with them. There have been times when someone was not doing well, either personally or professionally and we were able to intervene to help them. There have been other times when someone had a question that they really needed to ask and just by being available we are able to help.

We encourage you to not sit in your office; the emails and other work can wait. Instead, enjoy the school you are so proud of by committing to daily "drives" around the campus. You just never know what you might see or hear!

Instructional Leadership: How many brief, encouraging sticky notes can you leave in teachers' classrooms this week complimenting them on something you saw them do during a lesson? Not a "good job" but a real compliment on something you observed. Nothing formal, but authentic.

Servant Leadership: Challenge yourself to ask a question of each staff member this week. It could be about their family or their favorite candy bar, but write down what you hear for later reference (or surprise them sometime with their favorite!).

What Am I Learning? Write down three things you learned this week about your staff that you did not already know.

Tell Your Story: Have you ever considered video recording your strolls through the hallway and adding commentary? How might you use such a recording to spread good news?

Reflections/Celebrations: How does knowing about your team's personal lives help you become a more reflective leader? Reflect on your personal style. Would your staff answer the same way?

WEEK 40: KAIZEN

"We cannot become what we want to be by remaining what we are."
- Max DePree

The premise of this book has remained a simple one. We want to help all campus administrators get a little better and we believe that by sharing our stories, insights, and questions you might be able to do just that. Dramatic, impactful change rarely happens suddenly. Effective and sustainable growth generally evolves over time, with small and incremental steps. The activities and questions we have shared can, and should be, adjusted to meet your needs but the concepts behind them are constant characteristics of successful campus administrators. To become a well-rounded leader, you will be called upon at any given moment to be a(n):

- Instructional Leader
- Servant Leader
- Learning Leader
- Lead Storyteller
- Lead Reflector/Celebrator

The Japanese have a word for continuous improvement or for

small incremental steps to success, *kaizen*. Successful organizations all over the world have used the principles of *kaizen* to build sustainable action plans and guide their work. In addition to the concept of continuous improvement, the philosophy of *kaizen* has evolved to include ideas that translate into simple, small solutions that, over time, have a large impact towards change.

In a school building that embraces *kaizen*, all stakeholders will strive to get a little better every day. As the lead learner in the building, you should constantly be the first to seek and learn about your school and ways to improve yourself as a leader. It does not matter where you are right now or where you have been, all of us can get better and that is exactly our goal: continuous improvement.

We hope this book has helped you reflect on your own leadership, given you actionable items to adjust and make your own, and most of all, that you have embraced the idea of improving a little bit each and every day. Thank you!

Instructional Leadership: In what areas do you believe you have improved the most as an instructional leader in the past school year?

Servant Leadership: Do you believe your staff sees you as a servant leader? Why or why not?

What Am I Learning? What are your next steps as a school leader? What do you need to know or be able to do that will improve your skills?

Tell Your Story: What are some words of wisdom you would share with a brand-new principal about the importance of the role?

Reflections/Celebrations: What are three amazing things that happened at your school in the past year? How can you recognize and celebrate these accomplishments with others?

ABOUT THE AUTHOR:
ROBERT THORNELL

Robert Thornell, Ed.D. did not get into education to be a principal. In fact, when he began his career as a self-contained fourth grade teacher, his main aspiration was simply to help kids. He likes to share that his dream was "to be one of those teachers that had the same classroom for twenty-five years and kids would come back to visit." Having moved around a lot as a child (ten schools in twelve grades), the importance of quality teachers and principals was not lost on him even in his formative years. Rob remembers wanting to be a teacher in second grade simply because he thought he could do a better job.

As years went by, Rob was fortunate to work with many wonderful educators and mentors. Many of those encouraged him to use his skills to help others and make schools better by becoming a campus administrator himself. It was this encouragement and guidance that paved the way for a successful career as a campus principal and then a move to district level positions to work with educational leaders in various capacities. It is these experiences and influences that were the catalyst for this book.

Rob earned his bachelor's degree from Texas Tech University and his master's degree in education administration from the University of North Texas. He later earned his doctorate in education administration from Baylor University. His research and dissertation revolved around the importance of mentorship of the first-year campus administrators. His greatest professional passion remains working with educational leaders as a colleague and a mentor.

Rob's campus administrative experience includes serving as the principal of Chisholm Trail Middle School. Under his leadership, this Title One school was named a "National School to Watch" by the National Association of Secondary School Principals (NASSP) in 2012. He also has served as an elementary school principal as part of his growth and development.

Rob has previously served as Deputy Superintendent in Northwest ISD (near Fort Worth, Texas) in which he oversaw multiple departments and deepened his belief that the role of a principal was even more difficult and complex than many imagine. Prior to this, Rob also was assistant superintendent for curriculum and instruction with a focus on instructional leadership and vast experience with professional learning communities.

Rob currently works as Director of Leadership Development in Lewisville ISD (Lewisville, Texas) as well as his collaboration with the non-profit organization, SchoolRubric, as its Director of Organizational and School Leadership. His work in the last few years has revolved around mentoring and developing school leaders to enhance education for all.

He is an active member of the Association for Supervision and Curriculum Development (ASCD), Learning Forward, Phi Delta Kappan, and Texas Association of School Administrators (TASA). He is a past state board of director of Texas ASCD as well as a certified trainer for the National Institute of School Leadership (NISL), a program designed for transformational school leaders, and is a graduate of the Texas ASCD Curriculum Leadership Academy. A true educator at heart, he has presented at the state and national level on topics ranging from professional development to education transformation.

ABOUT THE AUTHOR:
CHARLES WILLIAMS

Charles Williams never intended to be an educator. As a graduate of Purdue University with a degree in Communication and English, he accepted a job within his former school district as a public relations specialist. That job ultimately transformed when he was asked to step in to teach an English class and quickly fell in love with teaching.

With his newfound passion, Charles returned to school to pursue a transition to teaching degree and remained to earn a Master's in Teaching from Calumet College of St. Joseph. He began his official teaching career working with English Language Learners (ELLs) and even had the opportunity to work alongside his former 5th grade teacher at his former elementary school. Charles transitioned to teaching English Language Arts (ELA) for middle school and high school students at both district and charter schools. It was then that he decided to pursue an administrative role and completed a Master's in Educational Leadership from Purdue University.

During his final year of teaching, Charles was asked to also serve as the interim assistant principal for the middle school and was subsequently promoted to that position during the summer. While in this role, he had the opportunity to visit China through the Confucius Institute to establish partnerships and learn from middle and high schools. It was during this trip that he learned about the resignation of his principal and was encouraged to pursue the role.

Charles was reluctant as he only served one year as an assistant principal and did not feel qualified to assume the role of principal. However, at the urging of colleagues and mentors, he applied and was named as the new principal of the high school. Unfortunately, his career would have a rocky beginning. Because of the board's decisions to manage their own schools, he spent his first three years at three different schools. Despite the frustration of moving from location to location, he was able to gain valuable experiences that he would later implement at his third and current school.

Charles has been the principal of Plato Learning Academy, a charter school for kindergarten to Grade 8 students in Chicago, for the past five years. The school was initially identified as a failing school and was placed on the closing list prior to his principalship. His first year taught him a valuable lesson that would become a foundation for the remainder of the work. In an attempt to "fix" the school, Charles initially took a textbook approach by focusing on replacing the programs within the school thinking that an updated curriculum would resolve the low academic performance. It did not. The following year, Charles and his team focused on Social-Emotional Learning (SEL) as they wanted to ensure that the staff and students felt comfortable and supported. Everything changed. Attendance increased. Test scores increased. And the school was removed from the closure list and continues to thrive.

Charles has since expanded his work beyond his principalship. Following several speaking and training engagements, he launched his educational consulting company, CW Consulting. Through personalized keynotes, workshops, and trainings, he aims to unlock the potential within organizations.

During the pandemic, Charles capitalized on working from home by launching The Counter Narrative Podcast, a weekly show designed to challenge the often dominant narratives that negatively portray our already disenfranchised populations by interviewing educators from around the world and sharing personal reflections.

Charles also co-hosts an EduShow with one of the co-authors of this book, Michael McWilliams. Inside the Principal's Office is intended to create a safe space for educational leaders to connect, learn, and grow from one another.

ABOUT THE AUTHOR: MICHAEL MCWILLIAMS

Michael L. McWilliams decided he would become a principal when he was in the sixth grade because of the impact of his teacher, Mrs. Thelma Brown, and a community of adults who consistently conveyed the importance of education to him. Once a struggling learner, his desire has been to impact children in the same way he was impacted by his village of support. His life's mission is to empower others to become the best version of themselves through leading learning, casting vision and creating systems that promote growth and challenge the status quo.

Michael's career spans 26 years with 20 of them as a part of an administrative team. He spent one year as a Title I Parent Education Trainer and three years as a 6th grade teacher before being promoted to assistant principal. After serving two years in this role, he received his first opportunity to lead a school as principal. Currently, he serves as the lead learner and principal of Savannah Elementary School, a pre-kindergarten through 5th grade school, located in Aubrey, Texas. Under his leadership, the school has been recognized as a Professional Learning Communities at Work Model School by Solution Tree, an Imagine Math School of excellence for three years, and an Imagine Math Beacon School. In addition, Savannah Elementary also earned recognition as an exemplary school and recognized school by the Texas Education Agency.

In addition to his responsibilities as an elementary principal he is also a certified Gallup Strengths Coach and an educational presenter specializing in laying the foundation for effective implementation of the PLC at Work® process. His focus is on creating systems that close the knowing-doing gap, campus improvement planning, and creating a culture of collective responsibility. Equipping and empowering others to be the best version of themselves is his life's mission.

Michael founded The Learning Leader Educational Consulting in 2020. This has given him the opportunity to mentor aspiring administrators, coach existing principals and lead workshops nationally. He also serves as the co-host of *Inside the Principal's Office*, a bimonthly SchoolRubric leadership EduShow. He and his co-host, Charles Williams, endeavor to use this platform to build a collaborative environment and safe space for school leaders to connect, grow and learn together.

Michael earned a bachelor's degree in political science and master's degree in educational leadership from The University of Texas system. He is currently pursuing his Ed.D in leadership from the American College of Education.

Michael has been married to his wife, Shanda for 27 years. Together, they have two children, Kenan and Kennedy.

Made in USA - Kendallville, IN
13242_9781737864301
02.24.2022 1436